THE HISTORY OF LINCOLN HILLS GOLF CLUB
ONE MAN'S PERSPECTIVE

BY

JOHN R. CARNEY MD

&

R. J. RATHSACK

2009

Copyright © 2009 Richard Rathsack
All rights reserved.

ISBN: 1-4392-2005-0
ISBN-13: 9781439220054

Visit www.booksurge.com to order additional copies.

TABLE OF CONTENTS

Preface. 1
Chapter I – Early history of Mason County. 7
Chapter II – Stevens T. Mason and the "war" with Ohio 11
Chapter III – The Formation of Epworth Heights,
the Dummy Line/L&N RR 15
Chapter IV – The Beginning of Golf in Mason County 25
Chapter V – The Formation of the Lincoln Hills Golf Club. 31
Chapter VI – The New Clubhouse. 37
Chapter VII – Watering the Fairways 41
Chapter VIII – Alterations to the Clubhouse 47
Chapter IX – Golf Course Alterations 53
Chapter X – Employees of the Club. 59
Chapter XI – The By-Laws and the Board of Directors 65
Chapter XII – The Course Renovation of 2000. 69
Chapter XIII – Membership. 75
Chapter XIV – Tournaments and Champions 81
Chapter XV – Caddies 89
Chapter XVI – Disasters on the Golf Course. 95
Chapter XVII – Wagers 99
Chapter XVIII – Memories and Musings on the Past 105
Chapter XIX – In Summary 115
Appendices
    A. Timeline of Events 117
    B. The Founding Fathers of Lincoln Hills 120
    C. Lincoln Hills Golf Club Presidents. 123
    D. Club Champions. 125
    E. The Ten Commandments of Golf 128

JOHN R. CARNEY MD & R. J. RATHSACK

PREFACE

As I look from the clubhouse out over the immaculate green fairways, the rolling hills and the lovely trees of the Lincoln Hills Golf Club, I am filled with wonder. I can hardly believe that this beautiful and enjoyable golf course could have evolved from such a humble origin. I often think about the people who had a part in the founding of the club and about the many who were involved in its continual improvement.

I know that even the members of the board of directors of the club have no conception of the way this club was formed or appreciation of the obstacles which were overcome in its development and survival. They seem to think that it was always the way it is now, sort of like being born fully developed. This is our reason for writing this book. Understanding the history of the club may give the reader more appreciation for what we have, more concern about the financial status of the club, and more determination that the club remain viable and financially secure in the future. This is a relevant concern when one considers the number and quality of the golf courses with which Lincoln Hills must compete in this Twenty-First Century.

The present Lincoln Hills Golf Club was considered in 1918, planned in 1920, and opened in August of 1921, the year and month of my birth. I first played the course in 1934, and it was a pitiful thing. It was brownish white in color. The turf in the fairways and the rough was the same, except that the fairways were more closely mown. Both consisted of isolated clumps of grass set in a sandy base. These clumps of grass were called tussocks, sometimes pronounced "tusks". A W. "Fred" Church, the early long-time president of the club was remembered as complaining that his ball "was lying on its side behind a tusk".

Because of these conditions it would have been almost impossible to play by "summer rules". In those days a player placed his ball on the back edge of a tussock and tried to pick it off cleanly without hitting the ground first. If he did indeed hit the turf, the ball didn't travel far and it made his hands ring. In the rough where a golfer was not allowed to move his ball, he had to strike it with a sharply descending blow to get it out from between the clumps or he wouldn't get much distance out of the shot. This type of stroke was rarely played on other courses.

Otto A. "Bub" Starke Jr. in his treatise on Lincoln Hills described the fairways in the first years of the club as kept narrow to eliminate excessive mowing, and he described the rough as uncut and knee-high. He wrote that if a player hit his ball into the rough in those days, the only recovery was to take a niblick, which was the equivalent of a nine-iron, and try to get the ball back into the fairway.

My family came to camp at the Ludington State Park each year beginning with its opening in 1934 and my Father and I often played golf at Lincoln Hills. Although I loved golf, I had to be urged to play there, because the course was a wasteland. My Father loved it even then, and it would be a treat for me to have him return to life for a day, if only to marvel at the course's transformation.

The basic layout of Lincoln Hills remained the same as it was first planned until the alterations of 2000, when the nines were reversed, two new holes were built, and two others were drastically changed. Although the sequence of the holes did not change, the original course was much shorter than the present one. The course was lengthened a little at a time, as many of the tees and greens were moved. The original layout had a par of 67. As the holes were lengthened, par went to 68, 70, and with the alterations of the year 2000 to 72.

The original greens were very small since there was at that time little money available to build, mow, and maintain larger ones. Because the greens were so small, they were not easy targets for a full shot. I played a round with another golfer in the 1950s in which he shot 71 while hitting only one green in regulation. He chipped in three times in the first four holes from a distance of only a few feet. Bunkers were in many cases little rudimentary strips of sand around the greens, no more than a yard or two wide. Some of them were located so far from the greens that they rarely came into play.

Through the years every hole has been changed and improved. During some years the alterations were extensive. The rest involved moving, enlarging or changing a green, moving or enlarging a tee, building or improving a bunker, or planting trees. All but two of the changes were made by our regular greens crew and without the club incurring significant debt.

The grass on the greens was originally fescue. The greens were not as closely mown as they are today and putting was uncertain. Bent grass was introduced to the greens in 1954. Bub Starke described the early greens as "magnificent, according to the standards of the day", but they were far less true than our present ones. Our smooth and manicured surfaces are the result of long years of labor and care and the addition of state-of-the-art mowers and other equipment.

The original tees were small and had worn and uneven surfaces. Because they were so tiny, the turf had no chance to recover from overuse, and part of their surface area was generally bare of grass. During the major alterations of 2000, improvements were made to most of the tees. Their surfaces were enlarged and smoothed and alternate tees were built on most holes. Enlarging the teeing grounds made it possible to move the markers frequently and avoid excessive turf wear. The erection of multiple tees made the course more playable for golfers of different skills.

The original course was not engineered the way new courses are today, and very little dirt was moved in the original construction. The little moguls in the fairways which are a characteristic of the course were not planned. It was just the way the land was formed. Many of the little swales which formerly made fairway mowing uneven have gradually filled in over the years.

One effect of these constant alterations and improvements was that during most years, while construction was going on, we were forced to use closely mown spots in one or more fairways as temporary tees or greens. The course was seemingly always a work in progress.

Someone wrote that history begins when the last person who knew what actually happened is dead. We can certainly say that we are recording history when we describe the origin of Lincoln Hills, because everyone involved in its beginning died long ago. Most of the members who were responsible for the early improvements to the course are also gone. My partner in this enterprise and I have

THE HISTORY OF LINCOLN HILLS GOLF CLUB: One Man's Perspective

tried to interview and jog the memories of the older members in writing this history. This has not always been successful as memories fade and names and dates and even facts pass into oblivion.

Occasionally we have come upon discrepancies in this history, most of which we have been able to resolve. But the word "story" is in the word "history", and through the years stories have the habit of changing.

Lincoln Hills' history is a part of the history of the Ludington area and is intimately involved with the history of Epworth Heights. In order to put the founding, the development and the events of the club into perspective, we have included information about the history of Michigan, Mason County, Epworth Heights and the Ludington and Northern Railroad.

I am doing most of the writing of this book, while my partner, Dick Rathsack, is doing most of the research. Our interests and talents complement one another. Dick is a past president of the Mason County Historical Society. He has made a study of the history of Mason County and Epworth Heights, which has been invaluable in putting this book together. He has searched the internet, delved into courthouse records, reviewed documents in the research library at White Pine Village, and pored through old newspaper files.

We also relied on the minutes of the Lincoln Hills Golf Club; the brief "Lincoln Hills Golf Club, An Historical Review", written by Bub Starke; "Looking Back Eighty Years of Golf at Epworth" by Betty Truxell; and "Steps to the Heights" by Helen Putnam Shaver; a series of articles written about the club by F. B. Olney, A. W. Church, and Harold King and published in the Ludington Daily News on July 22, 1931; the "General History of Michigan" published by Charles Richard Tuttle in 1873; and "An Illustrative History of The Great Lakes State", published by Windsor Publications in 1987. We are indebted to Russ Miller for aid in securing pictures and to Lincoln Hills for permission to copy them. We are also indebted to Epworth Heights for further pictorial aid.

We consulted with long-time club members Jack Rasmussen, Bob Erickson, Kim Berger, Garth Belland, and Dick Meissner. We are indebted to Cassius Street, a Lansing attorney and long-time Epworth resident, for his detailed research concerning the L&N

railroad, much of which we have repeated verbatim. I am grateful to my sister, Frances Carney Gies, a much-published author, for her corrections, suggestions and advice.

Since we began researching and writing this book, we have come across information of which I had either no inkling or only the sketchiest concept. Men like Stevens Mason, Charles Mears, and Justus Stearns, who were just names have taken on heroic proportions. This entire project has been an education to me.

There is a moral in this story, which will not be difficult to discern. Like golf itself, this book is a serious business. But, like golf, it is also supposed to be fun. I hope that you will be both instructed and entertained, and if parts of it are too earthy for your taste, you will skip on to something more palatable.

John R. Carney MD

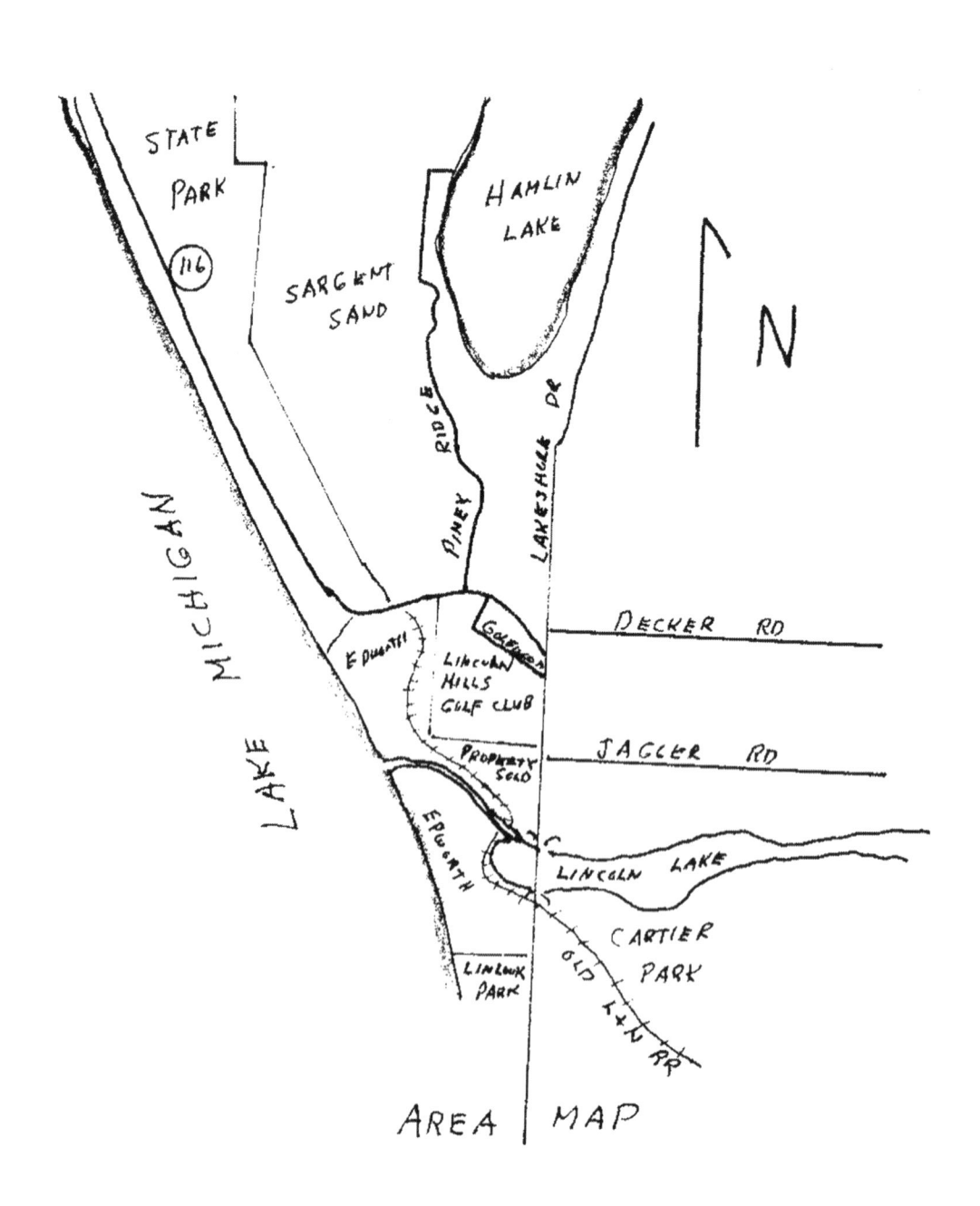

CHAPTER I
EARLY HISTORY OF MASON COUNTY

The first inhabitants of Western Michigan were Indians. They had numerous settlements along the rivers. The Michigan Territory was established by the Northwest Ordinance of 1787. Michigan was admitted into the Union as a state in 1837 and the western part of the state was politically partitioned by the legislature in 1840. The area we are concerned with was first called Notipekago County and later Ottawa County.

The earliest white settlers were fur traders and the first of them was William Quevillon. When the supply of furs ran out, lumbermen made their appearance during the mid 19th Century. They established logging camps and sawmills throughout the area, and they used the rivers to transport the logs and the lumber. By all accounts, lumbering was a rough and dangerous life.

Burr Caswell first permanent white settler in Mason County.

The first permanent white settler in the area was Burr Caswell who arrived in 1840 and established a home in the Buttersville area which later became the first county seat. The courthouse still stands in White Pine Village and is located about 100 feet from its original site. Quevillon operated the first post office in the area, and this log structure is also now located in White Pine Village.

Charles Mears (1814 – 1895)
began his lumbering exploits in 1836.

Charles Mears acquired huge tracts of land in Western Michigan between 1841 and 1855 by purchasing them from the United States Government, and he and others like Justus Stearns, Antoine Cartier, Delos Filer, Michael Danaher, James Ludington, and Eber Ward bought and lumbered large tracts in the area all around Ludington.

In 1855 Ottawa County was divided into Oceana, Mason and Manistee Counties. Mason County was named after the State of Michigan's first governor, Stevens Thomson Mason, a Virginian who was first appointed by the United States Government as Governor of the Michigan Territory before it became a state. Mason was only 23 at the time of his appointment and 25 when he was elected Governor of the new State of Michigan. He waged a "war" with the State of Ohio over the boundary between the states which we will describe in detail in Chapter II, and he was a hero in Michigan.

Mason County was subdivided into three townships, Pere Marquette in the south of the county, Little Sable in the middle, and Free Soil in the north. These townships were established so that each of them included one of the three rivers of the county, the Pere Marquette, the Little Sable, and the Big Sable. These were the only routes of transportation available in the area at that time. Transportation north and south was along the coast of Lake Michigan by boat.

It is a curious fact that most of the rivers in Western Michigan form lakes where they empty into Lake Michigan. Hamlin Lake is artificial, having been created in 1859 by Charles Mears who built the dam in the Big Sable River which is the precursor of the one that is located in the Ludington State Park. The dam washed out in 1888 with devastation of the town of Hamlin below it and collapsed again in 1912. Most of the other Michigan shoreline lakes are natural. These lakes have generally been the sites of the Western Michigan cities and towns such as Saugatuck, Douglas, Holland, Grand Haven, Whitehall, Montague, Muskegon, Pentwater, Ludington, Manistee, Onekama, Arcadia, Frankfort, and Charlevoix, all of which are situated at the outlets of these lakes.

The three Mason County rivers were no exception and the towns of Pere Marquette, Little Sable and Big Sable were located near the sites of the channels where water from the three lakes flowed into Lake Michigan. The town of Pere Marquette was located on the north bank of Pere Marquette Lake. Little Sable was on the north bank of the Little Sable River just south of what is now the Lincoln Hills Golf Club. Big Sable was on the north bank of the Big Sable River just below the dam.

The natural channels of exit of all three lakes were altered by Charles Mears in order to facilitate the transfer of logs and to make shipping more convenient. Mears moved the exit of Big Sable Lake from its original outlet to its present site at the entrance to the Ludington State Park. The natural channel had the same origin at the dam, but meandered northward along the Lake Michigan shoreline toward Big Sable Point before emptying into the big lake.

Mears moved the exit channel of the Little Sable River from its original site south of the hill in Epworth to its present location north of the hill and just south of Lincoln Hills Golf Club. A lagoon remains in Epworth as a remnant of the old path of the river to Lake Michigan. In 1860 Mears closed the channel exiting Pere Marquette Lake at its site near Buttersville Park and moved it to its present location by the Coast Guard Station. There was considerable opposition to this move by the populace of the Buttersville area, but Mears had gotten to Washington first and he prevailed.

Charles Mears was influential in Washington, and as a great admirer of President Abraham Lincoln and his Vice-President Hannibal Hamlin, he changed the names of the towns of Little Sable to Lincoln and Big Sable to Hamlin. He operated sawmills and shingle mills at both towns.

Through his influence the name of Big Sable Lake was changed to Hamlin Lake and that of Little Sable Lake was changed to Lincoln Lake. At the same time the Little Sable River was also named the Lincoln River. The Big Sable River's name remained unchanged. Confusingly, a group of lakes draining into it are called the Sauble Lakes and there is a Sauble Junction in the area. Perhaps this discrepancy results from the French pronunciation of Sable. The Au Sable River in Eastern Michigan is pronounced something like "Aw Sobble".

Mears arranged to have the county seat moved from the Buttersville area to Lincoln in 1861. Through the influence of James Ludington the name of the town of Pere Marquette was changed to Ludington in 1861 and the county seat was moved there in 1867. Both Lincoln and Hamlin became ghost towns as the lumber ran out and the industry disappeared.

Railroads came to Mason County starting in 1873, when the Flint and Northern Railroad was extended to Ludington. Spurs were built to reach the northern parts of the county. The railroads were an aid to the lumbering business and towns were erected along the rail lines. Scottville and Custer have endured. Many of the others became ghost towns. A town was erected at Victory Corners on the rumor that the railroad would pass through there. When the line was laid well south of there, the town disappeared almost overnight.

Sawmills, that the lumbermen operated, frequently burned to the ground leaving more ghost towns in their wake. Some of these, located near the outlet of Pere Marquette Lake, were named Taylorville, Setonville, and Buttersville. As the supply of lumber waned in the late 19th Century and the country was in a depression, local leaders began to look about for other sources of revenue and industry. They considered tourism as a possible partial solution to their problem.

CHAPTER II
STEVENS T. MASON AND THE "WAR" WITH OHIO

This chapter is a digression, but it explains the popularity of Governor Stevens T. Mason and why our county was named after him. It probably explains the animosity towards Michigan by certain Ohioans, an animosity handed down from generation to generation. Perhaps as a result of this, people like Ohio State's football coach Woody Hayes refused to speak the word Michigan, but referred to the University of Michigan as "that school up north". It may also explain why Michigan motorists should not speed through Ohio. Their state police are said to be especially on the lookout for enemy Michigan transgressors.

Stevens T. Mason

Stevens T. Mason (1811 – 1843)
First Governor of Michigan for whom
Mason County was named.

Michigan was a territory and became a state in 1837 when it was first able to prove a population of over 60,000 as required by law. Ohio was already a state with a population of over a million. The demarcation line between the states was set by the Northwest Ordinance of 1787 which allocated to the Michigan Territory all lands north of a line running east from the southern end of Lake Michigan and terminating at the shore of Lake Erie.

Ohio, in its constitution and by an act of its legislature in 1835, claimed a strip of land north of this line, stealing an area five miles wide at its western end and eight miles wide at its eastern terminus at Lake Erie. The land was rich farmland but more importantly it included Toledo and the harbor of the Maumee River, giving Ohio a port on Lake Erie. Toledo wasn't much of a city in those days, but the port was crucial. The State of Michigan had purchased 1,000 acres of prime waterfront land in Toledo on which to build the University of Michigan. The line of demarcation that Ohio claimed was called the Harris Line. Michigan's claim was based on the Fulton Line. These were named after the men who surveyed them.

Robert Lucas (1781 – 1853)
served as the 12th governor of Ohio from 1832 to 1838.

The Secretary and Acting Governor of the Michigan Territory at the time of the Ohio steal was Stevens T. Mason. Mason was young but vigorous and he wasn't going to accept Ohio's theft without a fight. Ohio's governor was Robert Lucas, a much older man, more dignified, irascible, and perhaps pompous. Lucas, his commissioners and 600 men went to Perrysburgh to survey the Harris Line. They found Governor Mason, General Jacob Brown of Tecumseh and about a thousand men of the Michigan Militia waiting for them in Toledo. Governor Lucas backed off and contented himself with "watching over the border".

Later Lucas sent three commissioners accompanied by a large fully armed force to survey the strip in question and remark the Harris Line. Mason got wind of this. He directed the legislature to pass the Pains and Penalties Act, making it a criminal offense to exercise official functions or to accept office within the disputed strip. When the Ohio group arrived they found a superior force of Michigan Militia under General Brown waiting for them. Several Ohioans were arrested and the rest were put to flight in abject fear. This was the first victory of Michigan over the State of Ohio or over Ohio State, as we prefer to think of it.

However, the frightened Ohioans reported to their governor that they had been part of a mighty battle against a superior force and that a number of them had been killed or taken prisoner. Governor Lucas reported these claims as he protested vehemently to President Andrew Jackson, who then asked Governor Mason for his version. Mason replied that no shot was fired, no blood was shed and that the Ohioans made "very good time of it as they fled through the cottonwood swamps leaving hats and clothing behind".

There was huge excitement over this event in Ohio and a special session of the Ohio legislature was called. An act was passed to prevent the forcible abduction of Ohio citizens, and the act authorized the courts to hold session in Toledo on September 7, 1835.

Meanwhile, Michigan sheriffs were arresting Ohio officials who attempted to function in the strip. A Major Benjamin Stickney was arrested, but he refused to mount his horse to go to jail. When he was put on his horse, he got off. He was then put on his horse and two men walked beside him to hold him on it. When they tired of that, they tied his feet together with a rope passing under the horse's belly.

Major Stickney's son, called Two Stickney since his older brother was named One, resisted his father's arrest. He stuck a knife into the leg of the Monroe County sheriff and then escaped back into Ohio. It was the only blood shed in the "war" and Two Stickney was the object of continual unsuccessful petitions for his extradition to Michigan.

Governor Lucas was determined to save face by having a court session held in Toledo on September 7, as required by Ohio law. But his judges were warned of a major Michigan force waiting for them in Toledo and they were afraid to go. Eventually a brave officer led the frightened judges into Toledo at three o'clock in the morning. A schoolhouse was entered and a two minute court session was held. Then they all high-tailed it back to Maumee, Ohio.

President Jackson was upset by this friction between the states and he courted the Ohio electoral vote in the upcoming presidential election. He ordered the states to stop their quarreling and despite an opinion by the United States Attorney General that Michigan was in the right, President Jackson suggested that the decision as to which state owned the strip be left to the citizens involved. Governor Mason disregarded these orders, and he was replaced by the President as Secretary and Acting Governor of the Michigan Territory. This order was also largely ignored.

But Ohio had the last word. When Michigan applied for statehood in 1837, a condition was made by President Jackson that the Harris Line would prevail, and Ohio would get Toledo and the rest of the strip. The University of Michigan had to give up its Toledo site and move to Ann Arbor instead. To compensate for their loss, Michigan received the rocky western part of the Upper Peninsula. The heroic Stevens T. Mason was then elected as the first Governor of the State of Michigan. He died in 1843 at the age of 31.

CHAPTER III
THE FORMATION OF EPWORTH HEIGHTS
THE DUMMY TRAIN AND THE L&N RAILROAD

A brief history of Epworth Heights is integral to any discussion of the history of the Lincoln Hills Golf Club for many reasons. The sites of the two areas are contiguous. The approach to the course area was originally by way of the Epworth grounds. At least half of the founders of Lincoln Hills were Epworth residents. The design of the original golf course was largely prepared by Thomas Gatke of Epworth. Epworth members have been a continual sustaining part of the Lincoln Hills membership and a support of the dining room.

There have been many occasions when bargains have had to be struck when there were mutual or conflicting interests between Epworth Heights and Lincoln Hills. Principally, conflicts arose over the strip of land which separates the two. Sometimes feelings were hurt on one or both sides. But it is certain that Lincoln Hills could not have achieved its goals without Epworth support and that the Epworth experience has been enhanced by having Lincoln Hills so close to its doors. Friendly cooperation between the two was obviously of great benefit to both parties.

At the end of the lumbering era the influential citizens of Ludington were desperately looking for another source of industry to keep Ludington from turning into another ghost town. A Citizen's Development Company was formed which started new industries on the north side of Ludington. Officers of the Flint and Pere Marquette Railroad looked into the possibility of attracting the Big Rapids branch of the Epworth Assembly, a two week annual get-together of Methodists whose purpose was spiritual and educational, from its summer camp at Reed City to the area it now occupies on the shore of Lake Michigan north of Ludington.

The hill along the beach which is now a part of Epworth Heights had been the site of picnics for people going between Ludington and the town of Lincoln. Although lake front property was not highly valued in those days of hard work for survival and little time for recreation, it was recognized that the beach air might be a tourist attraction. The beach and the area around the outlet of the Lincoln River were strewn with logs, boards and debris, the residual of the logging industry. Later Epworth citizens collected and burned these logs in huge bonfires while cleaning up the area.

In 1894 The Citizen's Development Company and Epworth entered into a fifteen year agreement. Epworth was to continue its assembly at the chosen site on the bank of Lake Michigan and Justus Stearns and the Citizen's Development Company agreed to build Epworth a hotel, an assembly hall, board walks, a pier, and several cottages, which along with the land would go to Epworth without charge at the end of the fifteen years if Epworth fulfilled its part of the agreement by continuing to hold its summer assemblies there.

Justus Stearns (1845 – 1933) (Courtesy of the Mason County Historical Society).

The Citizen's Development Company also agreed to pay Epworth the sum of $21,000 plus $1,000 a year for that 15 year period. In return, the company received title to certain land south of the Lincoln River on Epworth property on which to build a power plant and to erect poles and electric lines. The purpose of the power plant was to electrify a proposed street railway between Ludington and Epworth Heights. Epworth was granted the right to build cottages on the company's land.

Justus Stearns built the agreed-upon hotel and other structures in a remarkably short period of time in order to get the area ready for the first assembly that summer. Many Ludington citizens built cottages at Epworth which they rented to Epworth attendees, and many Epworth people lived in tents at the early assemblies. The assemblies grew so popular that they became national rather than regional affairs.

In retrospect, this seems like an incredibly sweet deal for Epworth. The size and the variety of the benefits which they received without any monetary reciprocity on their part are amazing. The assessed value of the land which they were given scot-free is 30 million dollars. Their entire initial infrastructure was built and donated to them. They were paid a sum of money which inflation has made equivalent to nearly a million dollars. In return they held their annual religious and educational programs to which local people were invited.

Initially assembly attendees were ferried from Ludington to Epworth by boat, a courtesy of Justus Stearns. On February 19, 1895 Ludington city fathers organized the Epworth League Railway. At a meeting on March 9 they elected Frank Filer as president, F. B. Olney as secretary and George Stray as treasurer. At a cost of $8,000 for the tracks and $3,000 for the rolling stock, the company built a railroad spur from the corner of Dowland St. and Charles St. [now Rath Avenue] in downtown Ludington north along Charles St. to Bryant Road and then angled it northwest and terminated it at Epworth on the west bank of Lincoln Lake. Epworth sold the right-of-way through their property to the railroad for one dollar.

THE HISTORY OF LINCOLN HILLS GOLF CLUB: One Man's Perspective

The Epworth League Railway referred to by the locals as the "dummy train".
(Courtesy of the Mason County Historical Society)

Epworth passengers came to Ludington from their homes by way of the Flint and Pere Marquette Railroad, whose station was adjacent to that of the spur, and continued on to their cottages by way of the new line. The railroad offered a fare of a nickel to Epworth residents, and some were offered free travel. In the fall of 1900 Justus Stearns acquired a controlling interest in the railroad and on July 17, 1901 the Epworth League Railway was reorganized as the Ludington and Northern Railroad.

The steam locomotive on the spur was named the D. W. Parsons in honor of one of the founders of Epworth. It was an odd vehicle which looked more like a coach than an engine. One version of the origin of the line's nickname has it that the Ludington children used to exclaim, "Look, here comes that dummy train". Thus the railroad became known as the Dummy Line.

However, the dictionary defines "dummy" as "a locomotive furnished with condensing engines and, hence, without the noise of escaping steam." There is an old song about "The Dummy Line, come rain or shine", which is not about the Ludington area, so it appears that this was a generic term for a certain type of railroad. The first locomotive of the line was purchased from the Grand Haven Street Railroad. In 1901 a new engine was bought from the J. G. Brill Co. of Philadelphia.

The Dummy Line became the main method of transportation to Epworth. The building of the railroad made the proposed power plant on the Lincoln River unnecessary and the idea was dropped. Right-of-ways were purchased east of Hamlin Lake, and in 1901 the railroad was extended east of what is now Lakeshore Drive past the South Bayou to the Hamlin Lake Hotel. In 1906 it was further extended on northward to the south shore of Upper Hamlin Lake and in 1913 a spur was built north of the Lincoln River to accommodate Epworth people located on their north beach.

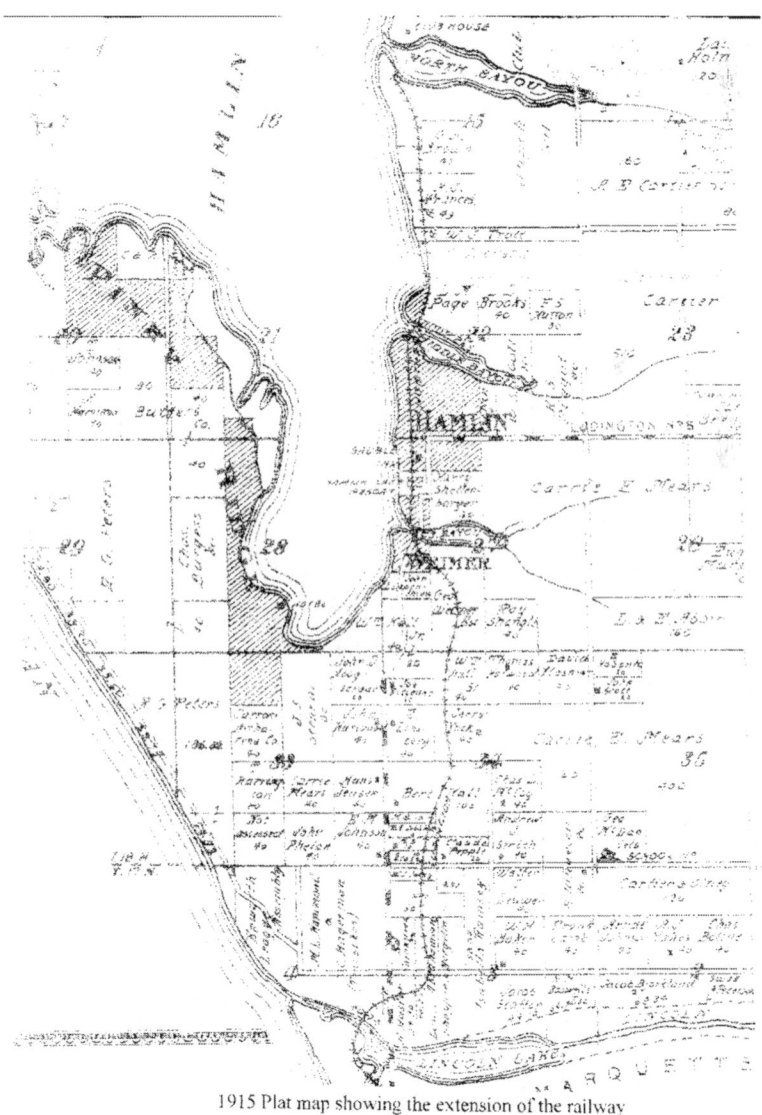

1915 Plat map showing the extension of the railway to south shore of upper Hamlin Lake.

Three years later a spur of the railroad was built through Epworth property and around what is now the Lincoln Hills golf course to the Piney Ridge area in order for the Hubbell Sand Co. of Pittsburgh to ship sand from that area. This became a major problem for Lincoln Hills in later years and will be discussed in detail in the chapter on club alterations.

Old Baldie, also called Mt. Baldie and Father Baldy, was a huge sand dune something like a smaller Sleeping Bear or the dune at Silver Lake, which extended from the area which is now south of M-116 along the area of the present 11th fairway across what is now M-116. It was estimated to be 350 feet in height. The Hubbell Sand Co. removed the entire northern part of Old Baldie, leaving a valley through which M-116 was built toward the Ludington State Park in 1932. When I arrived in Ludington in 1949, only the southern part of the dune remained.

The Dummy Line was closed in 1918 as the automobile became the general means of transportation, and the only traffic on it was the occasional sand train. Epworth wanted the tracks removed. In 1922 Epworth brought a law suit against Justus Stearns, the benefactor of Epworth and the principal owner of the railroad, to force the railroad to remove its unused tracks. The case was decided in the Michigan Supreme Court, which ruled that if the train was not in operation for a certain period of time, the owners could be forced to remove the unused tracks. On the last day before the removal could be enforced, the Dummy train was run up the line once more, voiding its closure.

In 1936, Epworth applied to the Interstate Commerce Commission to tear up the tracks. In the application the right-of-way through Epworth was to be returned to Epworth, while that through Lincoln Hills property was to go to Lincoln Hills. The judgment was not granted and the tracks and right-of-way were then sold by the railroad to the Sargent Sand Company.

The next year the Sargent Sand Company started operation, moving sand from the dunes north of Lincoln Hills to use in glass-works and for making molds in iron foundries. The railroad, generally called "The Sand Train", ran for many years hauling vast amounts of sand away. It was finally abandoned on January 15, 1982.

The public road from Ludington north to Epworth and to Lincoln was originally on the Lake Michigan beach. When Lake Michigan's waters rose, it was necessary to move the road inland, and Lakeshore Drive [first called Amelia Avenue] was built. The house at 601 N. Lakeshore Drive, a coach stop along the road, was also originally located on the beach, and it too was moved back away from the lake to its present site. This is the oldest frame house remaining in Ludington.

As part of the initial agreement, Epworth granted a public right-of-way through its grounds until a bridge could be constructed across Lincoln Lake as a continuation of Charles St. The people of Epworth, however were unhappy with the public traffic on their streets. When Lakeshore Drive was first built, it only extended as far as what is now Cartier Park. When the road approached Lincoln Lake, it ran through Epworth Heights coming out on the Lake Michigan beach south of the Epworth Heights Hotel. It continued along the beach and then left it near the Lincoln River, crossed the river by means of a bridge, and proceeded to the Lincoln Hills property and north to Hamlin Lake. This road was a sandy mess.

The extension of the road north past Epworth eventually came as an extension of Lakeshore Drive rather than of Charles St. and the bridge across Lincoln Lake where it is today dates to 1909, the year Epworth fulfilled its lease and came into possession of its grounds. When the bridge was completed it relieved Epworth of public traffic and later its entrance was constructed as it is today. In 1910 Antoine Cartier traded 73 acres of land on the beach north of the Lincoln River to Epworth for 80 acres of Epworth land across the highway, and he donated this land to the city as Cartier Park.

Lincoln Bridge north of Ludington about 1910. (Courtesy of the Mason County Historical Society)

In 1898 the Citizen's Development Company was unable to come up with its annual $1,000 contribution to Epworth. Epworth foreclosed on it hoping to realize the $1,000 payment. They forced the company to liquidate its property holdings in Epworth but realized only $438 as the company disbanded. Epworth not only lost the money, but also the friendship of many Ludington citizens who had contributed to Epworth's formation. In the early 1900s Bert Olney and George Cartier bought up quit claim deeds to the property and they ordered Epworth to vacate it. However a cottage had already been built, and another law suit followed, which Epworth eventually won in the Michigan Supreme Court.

In 1904 Olney and Cartier arranged at no charge for the Michigan National Guard to hold its annual summer training session at Camp Lincoln located at what was described as "the historic Lincoln Fields", the site of Lincoln Hills Golf Club. There is no indication in the records as to how or in what way the property was historic.

Michigan National Guard encamped at the Lincoln Fields from 1904 to 1912.
(Courtesy of the Mason County Historical Society)

Having the National Guard Encampment at the Lincoln Fields entailed the marching of soldiers through Epworth Heights, the only access to the property. These soldiers were generally regarded as shiftless heavy drinkers and hell-raisers. The Epworth settlers were not happy with the arrangement, and it was suggested that Olney and Cartier might have intended it as a means of getting even with Epworth for their court loss. Epworth citizens were terrified at having the soldiers so near and the commanding general agreed to "keep his soldiers off Epworth grounds if Epworth would keep its women off encampment grounds".

On August 14, 1907 a troop train ferrying troops from the encampment backed into the smaller Dummy Train coming south from Epworth with many serious injuries resulting. In the absence of a Ludington hospital, the injured were cared for in the homes of physicians or in those of public-spirited citizens. This catastrophic accident was the needed impetus for the formation of the first hospital in Ludington, and a few weeks later Justus Stearns donated his former home to a hospital association, and this became the first Paulina Stearns Hospital.

The Michigan National Guard continued to have its annual summer training camp at the Lincoln Hills site until 1912 when the operation was moved to Camp Grayling. Before the move Governor Osborn reviewed troops at Camp Lincoln, including infantry, cavalry, artillery, and an ambulance corps. The last encampment of the Michigan National Guard was held in 1915 at Camp Lincoln in conjunction with the New York National Guard. Fifteen thousand troops were assembled there on that occasion.

CHAPTER IV
THE BEGINNING OF GOLF IN MASON COUNTY

Golf was introduced into the United States from Scotland in 1887, when some golf clubs and balls were imported from the Old Country. A few men called "The Apple Orchard Gang" started knocking the balls around an orchard in Yonkers, New York, and in 1888 they formed the first permanent American golf club, The St. Andrews Golf Club.

In 1892 Charles Blair MacDonald designed and opened the first golf club in the Midwest as the Chicago Golf Club in Belmont, Illinois. This was a 7 hole course. Within two years the club was moved to its present location in Wheaton, and became the first 18 hole golf course in America. It remains as one of the greatest and most exclusive golf clubs in the world.

MacDonald, an American, had attended St. Andrews University in Scotland in the 1870s and had learned to play golf while studying there. He played several matches against the immortal "Young" Tom Morris, the St. Andrews professional and [British] Open Champion. In MacDonald's accounts of these matches, he seems to have been the original pigeon, having been beaten and plucked repeatedly by Tom Morris, but only by the smallest of margins. At any rate MacDonald was thoroughly bitten by the golf bug. He won the first official United States Amateur Golf Championship, was one of five founding members of the United States Golf Association, and designed some of the great golf courses of the world including the Chicago Golf Club, the National Golf Links on Long Island, the White Course at the Greenbrier, and the Mid-Ocean Club in Bermuda.

Betty Truxell, in her treatise on golf at Epworth Heights, stated that golf was introduced to Epworth in 1900 by Dr. Samuel Plantz, president of Lawrence College in Appleton, Wisconsin. Dr. Plantz petitioned the Epworth board for use of their land for the formation of a 7 hole golf course. He also asked for "a few loads of clay to be spread around the land and tamped down". The Epworth Quarterly reported six years later that "Epworth not only has a good golf links, but this season is to have a well-organized and efficiently officered golf club. Its name will be the Epworth Golf Club and its officers are A. L. Bentley, President, and H. L. Haskell of Ludington, Secretary". An annual fee of $10 entitled the payer to the use of the golf course, the tennis courts, and the croquet grounds. In 1907 twenty-five members were listed, including five from Ludington.

According to Helen Shaver, the combined Epworth and Ludington members raised enough money to import a Scottish golf course expert, H. David Wilson, to revise the Epworth course. He moved the first tee to the southwest corner of the Epworth grounds to make it convenient for a proposed new clubhouse which was to be built near that area.

Plans were drawn for a clubhouse in 1907, but no action was taken until 1912 when E. N. Fitch, a Ludington lawyer who lived nearby and who owned the property comprising Linlook Park, was persuaded to donate a segment of land, which included three lots, for the location of the clubhouse. These lots lay adjacent to the southern border of Epworth Heights and included Lake Michigan frontage. It was predicted that building a clubhouse in this location would enhance the value of the rest of the Linlook Park property owned by Fitch.

In 1913 at the instigation of William Rath, the princely sum of $13,000 was raised from the Ludington community and $3,200 from Epworth, and under Rath's supervision a clubhouse was built on this site. A condition of the donation of the land was that the clubhouse be maintained for at least a ten year period. The resulting organization was called the Ludington Country Club or the Ludington-Epworth Country Club. Epworth leased its golf links to it at no charge until 1924 when the Epworthians decided not to renew the lease and to control their nine hole course themselves.

Ludington-Epworth Country Club. (Courtesy of James Fay)

The new clubhouse was described in glowing terms as follows: "This splendid structure, the best public building in Mason County is located in Linlook Park, just over the line [south] from the Assembly grounds, directly on the Lake Michigan beach and of course, facing the golf course. The building is a modern structure with all the conveniences of a country club, including a large assembly hall, parlors with open fireplaces, dining room, kitchen, spacious porches on both east and west fronts, bowling alleys, gentlemen's and ladies' lockers, shower baths, etc.". Two double tennis courts were under construction. The bowling alleys were in the basement.

In 1914 golfing annual dues at Epworth were $10 or fees were 75 cents a day. The country club was run as a separate organization from the golf course and had a $25 yearly membership fee. The rules of membership of the country club were copied from those of the Royal and Ancient Golf Club of St. Andrews in Scotland where there is more than one club adjacent to the golf courses, and where anyone can play the golf courses, which are municipally owned, but only members and guests can enter the portals of the clubhouses.

I had occasion to play golf at the Old Course at St. Andrews on several occasions. Once I played the course with Dr. "Sandy" Matheson, a Scottish friend who later became a captain of the Royal and Ancient Golf Club, a rare and prized honor. Following the round we had lunch in the clubhouse of the R&A, and after lunch Sandy gave us the grand tour of the clubhouse which included the club room which contained a display case filled with impressive trophies.

The most remarkable trophy was a silver rod to which were attached by silver chains a great number of silver and gold replicas of golf balls, each donated by a former captain of the club upon his inauguration into office. Sandy explained to us that this trophy, which was unusually heavy by this time, was called "The Captain's Balls". The Scots are a ceremonious people and love tradition. Sandy told us that when each new member is initiated, part of the ceremony calls for the applicant to kneel and to kiss "The Captain's Balls".

To go back to the Ludington Country Club, it was "the scene of many gay gatherings and offered many opportunities for Epworth and Ludington people to interact socially". There was no gate at Epworth in those days. Many Ludington folks owned Epworth cottages and there was more social contact between Epworth and local people at that time than there is today.

William Rath of Ludington was the first president of the Ludington Country Club. He was succeeded by O. A. Starke, Sr., president of the Star Watchcase Co. On July 11, 1919 the capital stock was increased to $25,000 to raise funds to pay off indebtedness and to provide stock to sell to new members.

On November 17th, 1919 during a heavy storm the beautiful clubhouse burned to the ground. The cause was officially given as defective wiring, but there was a strong suspicion that vagrants may have invaded the vacant structure during the off-season, built a fire and accidentally destroyed the building.

A questionnaire was sent out to all members, and a majority of them elected to rebuild at the same site. On April 3, 1920 at a meeting of the club directors, E. C. "Pete" Hardy, the manager of the Morton Salt Co., and F. O. Widmark of the Widmark Lumber Co. were appointed as a committee to rebuild the clubhouse, and in early July, 1920 a new and less impressive clubhouse was erected in the same area. It was used continuously until the new clubhouse of the Lincoln Hills Golf Club was built in 1931.

The Ludington Country Club was officially dissolved in 1931, the club merged with the Lincoln Hills Golf Club, and the structure and lots went to the stewardship of Lincoln Hills. The building remained vacant for years. Offers were made to purchase it for use as a roadhouse, but were rejected by K. B. "Turk" Matthews, a Ludington attorney representing Lincoln Hills, as being against the interests of Epworth.

Because it was a Methodist establishment, Epworth was officially and aggressively dry, even though one of the continual challenges for Epworth dwellers was to surreptitiously get rid of their empties. It was said that religion would have achieved an ecumenical state when the Catholics ate meat on Friday, the Jews ate pork, and the Methodists drank in front of each other. At the age of ten I plagued my strict Methodist Aunt Susie by asking her whether she would drink a bottle of beer if it was offered to her when she was dying of thirst in the desert. Her answer was, "No! It would only make me thirstier!"

By the time of the eventual sale of the Ludington Country Club clubhouse, its debts and interest were $8,975.10. Creditors settled for $5,309.40. In 1940 the land and building were sold to Parker Francis of Kansas City for $6,500. This sum was used to liquidate the old club's debts and the residual went to Lincoln Hills. The property was later sold by Francis to Glen Hatfield, who resold it in 1976 to Harold and Lucy Cabe of Little Rock, Arkansas. They deeded the land to Epworth Heights and took a lease from Epworth on the house in return.

In 1913 Harry H. Webster was brought to Epworth as a golf professional on the high recommendation of the A. G. Spalding Co. and of Charles "Chick" Evans of Chicago. Chick Evans had a national reputation as an exceptional golfer and fine gentleman and later was the winner of the United States Open Championship. Evans and Francis Ouimet were the foremost amateurs in the United States in that decade.

Webster remained in the capacity of Epworth's professional at least through the 1923 season, and was mentioned by Bub Starke in his treatise on golf at Lincoln Hills as a professional and one of the early members of the Lincoln Hills club who made its success possible. It is likely that he was also employed by Lincoln Hills, perhaps in an advisory capacity since there is mention of a professional's fee of $225 as part of the golf club's initial expense in 1921.

CHAPTER V
THE FORMATION OF THE LINCOLN HILLS GOLF CLUB

In 1915 the United States was beginning to train soldiers for their possible entry into World War I. One small part in this was the formation of an Officer's Training Center for the United States Army in the Lincoln Fields, which had been the site of the previous Michigan National Guard maneuvers. The Stearns Estate leased these grounds to the army. A railroad spur had been built to the site for the use of the Michigan National Guard and it was used for the transport of cannons and other heavy equipment. The encampment consisted of "tents and rough wooden mess halls".

The Officers' Quarters were a large wooden building constructed on the hill which is now the 18th tee of the Lincoln Hills Golf Club. This edifice was described as "sumptuous, and it was the scene of many house parties during which the officers became better acquainted with the local area people". A firing range was set up near the northwest area of the tract, using the dune called Old Baldie as a backdrop for both ordinary gunfire and cannons. The encampment was abandoned by the Army in 1918 at the conclusion of the war and all the structures were torn down except the Officers' Quarters, which later became the first clubhouse of the Lincoln Hills Golf Club.

First clubhouse of the Lincoln Hills Golf Club. (Courtesy of Russ Miller Studios).

    The Epworth golf course had become crowded, and in 1918 a movement was started primarily by W. T. Culver, Henry Haskell, and Thomas Gatke to build a new and longer golf course on the Lincoln Fields. The land, originally purchased by Charles Mears in 1848, had undergone changes in ownership. Frank Olney, who had loaned the property to the Michigan National Guard, had sold the land to a trust which was a part of the Stearns Estate in 1914. It was first leased by the trust to Lincoln Hills on August 29, 1922, and on July 23, 1925 William L. Hammond and Clyde Hagerman, as trustees for the Stearns estate, sold the land to Lincoln Hills for $6,500. The right-of-way for the L&N railroad, established in 1916, was not included in the sale.

W. T. Culver, the first president of Lincoln Hills Golf Club.

Henry L. Haskell, inventor of the Carrom game board and founder of the Haskelite Co. as seen in 1917. (Courtesy of Jane Gray)

Other additions were made to Lincoln Hills property in 1927 as two plots were acquired through delinquent tax purchases and two more were deeded to the club, one as a gift of M. B. Danaher and H. L. Haskell and the other as a gift of W. T. Culver. From pictures taken at the time of the army encampment, it appears that the land in the Lincoln Fields was a sandy wasteland with little grass or foliage, not looking auspicious for the future development of a fine golf course.

THE HISTORY OF LINCOLN HILLS GOLF CLUB: One Man's Perspective

Most of the men who were involved with the planning of the new club were already members of the Ludington Country Club, and they were seeking a longer and more challenging golf course than the one available at that time at Epworth.

Helen Shaver in her book on Epworth history stated that "Ludington golfers had sacrificed their Lincoln Hills Golf Course to state and federal troops for seven years". There are other references to golf having been played at a nine hole course in the Lincoln Fields at an earlier time, but we could find no reliable documentation to substantiate this. The seven years described by Ms. Shaver would date the abandonment by the golfers as 1914. This suggests that golf was played there between 1912 when the Michigan National Guard moved away and 1915 when the army moved in.

The first 12 pages of the log, that documented the activities of the Lincoln Hills Golf Club when it was first formed in 1920, are missing without explanation, but probably contained the minutes of an original club whose operations were interrupted in 1915 by the arrival of the United States Army. We assume that these records were deleted in order to use the old log book, but also to make a fresh start with the newly organized club.

Articles of Association of Lincoln Hills as a non-profit entity were executed on September 21, 1920. Bylaws were formulated and directors were elected. Annual dues were set at $30 for active members, $20 for associate members, who enjoyed playing privileges but could not vote on club matters, and daily fees for non-members were set at $1.25, weekly rates at $6, and monthly rates $20.

The first recorded meeting of the present Lincoln Hills Golf Club occurred on August 23, 1921. W. T. Culver, an associate of the Stearns estate was named president. Harold King, an employee of the Stearns estate, was named secretary, and he fulfilled these duties for many years and later became the mayor of Ludington.

The new club had 71 members who each paid $100 to help get the club off the ground. Taking into account inflation since that time, this fee was roughly equivalent to more than $2,000 today. Additionally $13,000 in bonds was sold at 7% interest to obtain the money necessary to get the club off the ground. Other bonds were authorized in 1922, 1923, 1926, 1930, and 1931 for further improvements in the course and for the new clubhouse.

The initial membership consisted of approximately half Epworth people, and the rest were local. The golf course first comprised only nine holes. As it became crowded it was extended to eighteen holes in 1923. The layout of the course was largely planned and supervised by Tom Gatke, born in Ludington and a resident until he was about 18 when he moved to Chicago with his parents while the family continued to maintain an Epworth cottage. Tom's father, Charles Gatke, was a local contractor who built and owned a resort, the Hamlin Lake Hotel, located on a bluff between the North and South Bayous of Hamlin Lake. He was also the contractor who built the first Mason County Courthouse which was located in the City of Ludington and the Ludington City Hall.

Expenses listed for the laying out of the original course were:

Land - $1,100
Dirt for greens - $6,052.85
Seed and fertilizer - $6,976.10
Pipe and plumbing - $2,913
Equipment - $1,810
Labor - $11,532
Repairs to clubhouse - $1,459
Golf architect - $112
Professional - $225.

The layout of the course in 1923 was similar to the one we played until the alterations of 2000 changed the course. The chief difference in that initial layout was that with the clubhouse on what is now the 18th tee, that hole was then the 1st. What is now the 17th hole was then the 9th, and what is now the 2nd, was then the 10th. This arrangement lasted until 1931 when the new clubhouse was built.

Fescue grass was planted throughout the course to make the fairways and greens. Pete Hardy donated the pipe that was used to water the greens. Apparently the Ludington Water Department, which had moved their lines out to Epworth Heights, continued them on to Lincoln Hills. The greens were watered, but the rest of the course was not.

Fairways and greens were mowed by hand. Roughs were completely uncut in the early days and the grass was knee high. We found a note in the club log indicating that as late as 1942 Lincoln Hills paid an Epworth employee $2.50 an hour to bring his equipment over and mow the Lincoln Hills fairways. Apparently Lincoln Hills did not own a motorized fairway mower even at that relatively late date.

In June 1923 Lincoln Hills joined the Michigan Golf League with annual dues of $10, and in 1926 it joined the Western Golf Association with dues of $15. The Western Golf Association located in Chicago, which still runs the Western Open, the Western Amateur, and the Western Junior tournaments, and administers the Evans Caddy Scholarships, was a power in American golf during the 20s and 30s. Its policies were in disagreement with the United States Golf Association over both rules and amateur status and for a time were a threat to the authority of the USGA.

CHAPTER VI
THE NEW CLUBHOUSE

The first major alterations at the Lincoln Hills Golf Club occurred in 1931 when bonds were sold and a new clubhouse was built at the present site at a mortgaged cost of $21,000. The old Ludington Country Club had served it purpose, but it had become inadequate both in size and in amenities. With the increase in summer resident colonies in the area, a more luxurious building became necessary, and it was desirable to locate it adjacent to the 18 hole Lincoln Hills golf course. When this new clubhouse was built, the Ludington Country Club merged with Lincoln Hills, and the Ludington Country Club clubhouse was abandoned.

Lincoln Hills Golf Club clubhouse looking west from the golf course.
(Courtesy of the Mason County Historical Society)

There was a real difference in purpose between the Ludington Country Club and the new entity which was created after its merger with Lincoln Hills in the new clubhouse. The Ludington Country Club was a social club. It was built adjacent to a golf course, and many of its members played golf at Epworth or at Lincoln Hills. But dues were paid for social purposes only and golfing charges were separate from club charges. Furthermore, playing golf did not entitle one to enter or to use the clubhouse.

Lincoln Hills, however, remained a golf club, which with its joining with the Ludington Country Club offered expanded social amenities. But its dues, except for those paid by a small group of social members, included golf and were primarily for golf. Non-members who played golf there were entitled to use the clubhouse including the locker rooms and lunch room, but were not allowed to attend dinners or parties except as a guest of a member.

The committee which was appointed to plan and supervise the construction and furnishing of the clubhouse consisted of John W. Beiger, chairman, Elbert C. Hardy, B. Ostendorf, Robert L. Stearns, Walter H. Pleiss, Alfred W. Church, B. S. Wilcox, Mrs. Robert L. Stearns, Mrs. Karl B. Matthews and Mrs. Elbert C. Hardy.

Consideration was given to locating the new building at the previous clubhouse site at the present 18th tee. But in the end it was decided to build it on a location in the apple orchard 400 yards west, to take advantage of more available space and of the views of Lake Michigan, the Lincoln River, and the hills of Epworth Heights.

The old Lincoln Hills clubhouse became a storage shed and was used for that purpose for several years until it was deemed unsafe and was torn down. Since the new clubhouse was built near the previous 2nd tee the former second hole became the first hole and the former 18th hole became the tenth. Otherwise the sequence of the holes remained the same.

The gravel road to the new clubhouse continued on to the north side of it, ending in a parking lot which was located to the north of the clubhouse in the area of the present practice putting green. The new first hole was shortened because of the new structure and parking lot, as the tee was moved to the north.

Lincoln Hills Golf Club clubhouse looking northeast from the parking lot.
(Courtesy of the Mason Country Historical Society)

The new clubhouse was planned by an architect and built by Oscar Nelson, a highly regarded local contractor. Nelson was praised for his efforts, as he made suggestions which reduced the cost of construction and increased the "completeness" of the building. He did extra work without making extra charges.

The new building was from 30 to 50 feet wide and 152 feet long. Its most outstanding feature beside the view was the split native stone fireplace and chimney. The new clubhouse is the same one we still use, but it was smaller than it is today. The areas to the sides of the pillars in the present ballroom were unheated porches used only during the warmer weather, and their floor level was a foot lower than the ballroom itself. The bar area was much smaller and was furnished with wooden booths. The ladies' locker room was small and it and a small apartment were located upstairs. The latter became the living quarters for the club manager or the professional and was used as such for many years. Today it is office space. The men's locker room was smaller than it is today and was furnished with metal lockers.

The original road to the clubhouse was in rough shape and was the source of many complaints until the road was black-topped in 1949.

CHAPTER VII
WATERING THE FAIRWAYS

The implementation of a sprinkling system for the fairways and the financial dealings which preceded the project were unquestionably the most significant events in the club's history. I have described in the Preface the club's difficult fairway conditions and the isolated tufts of grass called tussocks. These conditions had not improved during the first 35 years since the founding of the club, but they were a fact of life, and since this was the only golf course in the area, we had to put up with them and make adjustments in our golf swings.

Many of us believed that the sandy soil was so poor that it was impossible to grow lush, smooth fairways. Yet as far back as 1945, minutes of the club reported an interest in acquiring a fairway watering system. This project was deferred because, with its huge bonded indebtedness, the club did not essentially own itself.

Bonds had been issued at various times in the past in order to have money to start the club and to pay for course improvements and for the new clubhouse. In 1936 two series of bonds were issued totaling $48,700 which were supposed to pay 7% interest. These bonds were still outstanding in the mid-1950s and no interest had been paid in all those years. Even without compounding, the interest owed on the bonds had risen to $57,245. Because of subsequent inflation this total debt would today be the equivalent of at least $2,000,000. The club officials knew that they could not afford to pay out this amount, and they were reluctant to make major improvements in the course or in the clubhouse as long as this obligation hung over their heads.

A somewhat similar situation occurred once in my medical practice. A patient was deeply depressed. In trying to ascertain whether he might be bi-polar, I asked him if he had had any period in his life when he could think faster and achieve more than

THE HISTORY OF LINCOLN HILLS GOLF CLUB: One Man's Perspective

usual. He said that he had indeed had such a period a few years before, that he had made a lot of improvements in the house in which he was living, and that he had even built a picket fence around it. I asked him if in retrospect there was anything unusual or bizarre about his actions. He said, "Yes, it wasn't my house!" For the same reason the Lincoln Hills membership was reluctant to make any significant improvements as long as it wasn't "their house".

A committee was formed to look into ways to rid the club of this debt. It was estimated at the time by the committee that 90% of the bonds were held by wealthy public-spirited persons interested basically in the success of the club, while 10% were in "adverse hands", meaning that they were held by someone who had purchased them expecting to make a profit. The Stearns estate was the primary bondholder.

The committee continued to press the bond-holders and eventually reached an agreement with them. The Stearns Estate and other wealthy bond-holders agreed to settle their bonds and the accrued interest for 10 cents on the dollar. Harold King, the secretary of the club, who had purchased the bonds as an investment, was paid 50 cents on the dollar.

The members of the club were overjoyed by this settlement. We could hardly believe the club's good fortune in getting relief from this crushing debt, and we all highly resolved that we would never allow such a state of indebtedness to occur again and that from that point onward we would see to it that the club lived within its means.

Once the deal was consummated and the club could free itself of the debt, the committee members set about raising the money not only to pay off the bond-holders, but also to install a sprinkling system.

The club had granted a right-of-way for M-116 across Lincoln Hills' property in 1932 so that the public could gain access to the Ludington State Park. The park was being built at that time by the Civilian Conservation Corps. M-116 was planned to be the southern leg of a new US-31 which was to go along the lake shore to

Manistee. But there was so much protest over this project by environmentalists and property owners that the plan was abandoned and the northern half was never built.

The committee platted the area north of the course along the north side of what is now called Golfwood Road and on both sides of M-116. According to Kim Berger, a long-time member who owned a clothing store, Roland "Bob" Palmquist was especially active in this project, making repeated trips to Lansing which probably involved DNR approval of the project, and working with Clay Olmstead, an attorney who ran the Register of Deeds office, to legalize the platting of the land. In 1953 the club had sold off the area occupied by the Styx Bar for $5,000.

The Sargent Sand Company offered to purchase the sand from what remained of Old Baldie for 1½ cents a ton, estimating that over a two year period the club would realize $10,000 on the deal. There was opposition to this, not only because of the removal of a beautiful natural scenic landmark, but there was also concern that removal of the dune would leave the course defenseless against the prevalent north winds. Nevertheless, over the next few years the dune sand was sold and Old Baldie disappeared. The lots along M-116 and along the north side of Golfwood Road were also sold in the late 1950s. The club thus became free of debt, owned itself, and had money in the bank for the watering project.

Meanwhile, Truman L. "Tom" Atkinson, the owner of the Atkinson Manufacturing Company, who was influential in club affairs, decided to experiment to determine whether with the application of water and fertilizer he could grow satisfactory turf on this sandy soil. A number of us made a contribution to Atkinson's experimental fund, and he used the money to put sprinkler heads along the 8th [now the 17th] fairway, using city water for the experiment. The results of the watering were phenomenal. Lush grass appeared and the tufts filled in rapidly.

THE HISTORY OF LINCOLN HILLS GOLF CLUB: One Man's Perspective

Truman L. "Tom" Atkinson club president 1948-1950. (Courtesy of Russ Miller Studios)

    Herman Yoder, an engineer employed by The Dow Chemical Company, was a golf enthusiast. He purchased one of the lots on Golfwood Rd. and built a house there. Yoder was able to purchase a large amount of pipe from The Dow Chemical Company's brine wells in Mt. Pleasant at little expense. He planned to place a pump at the Lincoln River in order to pump free river water into the proposed watering system. This arrangement would avoid the expense of purchasing the large amounts of city water which would have been needed to water the sandy fairways. In 1955 Yoder estimated that the pump and accessories would cost $2,230 and the sprinkling system would cost between $15,000 and $20,000.

    Betty Mascal informed us that her father, Frank Johnson, a Dow engineer working under Yoder's supervision, designed both the pump and the sprinkler system. He did this on Dow's time and at no expense to the club.

Herman Yoder club president 1957-1958. (Courtesy of Russ Miller Studios)

Bruce Kronlein tells us that he helped his father Clarence install the pump. Clarence was a pipefitter who was a golfing member at Lincoln Hills. It is Bruce's impression that his father did the work without charge, as his contribution to the improvement of the club.

While the new watering system was a blessing, it had some problems. The watering barely covered the fairways and rarely reached the rough. As the system aged there were frequent leaks which had to be repaired. It was necessary for employees to go to each sprinkler head to activate it in turn. Two employees spent their nights doing this for many years.

In 1979 the sprinkler system was renovated at a cost of nearly $150,000 by Spartan Distributors of Sparta, Michigan, distributors of Toro Irrigation Equipment. New pipe was laid. The pump at the Lincoln River was replaced by a larger one with more power. The system was automated so that with central controls the course could be watered without activating individual sprinkler heads, thus eliminating the need for the former watering employees. The previous watering system provided a 120 foot wide strip of coverage. The new system covered a 188 foot strip and included areas around the clubhouse not previously covered. Furthermore the entire watered area could receive ¼ inch of water in an eight hour period, whereas the previous system required two ten hour periods for the same coverage.

Herman Yoder remained chairman of the greens committee for many years. Engineers are a different breed of cat. Masters and Johnson, the famous sex experts, had a few things to say about engineers. One of their female clients, who married an engineer, described their wedding night. Her husband was under the sheets with a flashlight, checking everything out. Herman was like that at Lincoln Hills. He could not pass by a hole in the ground, a leak, or a repair without snooping out the problem.

One of the early greens chairmen at Lincoln Hills was Manierre Dawson. Dawson was responsible for the lengthening of the original second hole which became the first hole when the new clubhouse was built in 1931, and he was responsible for the removal of the hill which blocked the view of the new green. He remained as greens chairman for many years and implemented many of the yearly improvements to the course.

Dawson was born in Chicago in 1887, the son of an attorney who owned a farm near Ludington. He studied engineering at the Armour Institute in Chicago and worked as a draftsman in Chicago in the winters while summering at the family farm. He started painting as a youth and was one of the first abstract painters in the world, perhaps antedating the famous Kandinsky. In 1914 he retired from drafting and moved to the Mason County farm and became a rich fruit farmer. He was an early and influential, if somewhat unpopular, member of Lincoln Hills.

Dawson was not a very expert golfer, but he was the quintessential clubhouse lawyer. He was very authoritative and if he didn't know a rule, we suspected that he made one up. He called penalty strokes on his opponents on a regular basis. Some of us nicknamed him after a certain farm by-product similar to his first name. His wife Lillian was singularly humorless and she terrorized the lady golfers for years with her version of the Rules of Golf.

Dawson gave up painting for many years while he was making his fortune, but took it up again in later years. Herman Yoder and I made a golfing trip to Sarasota, Florida around 1960. Manierre was a winter resident there, and Herman prevailed upon me to go with him to pay Dawson a visit in the hope that he would sponsor us for golf at Sarasota Country Club. Our hints were fruitless, but during the call the painter showed us his latest abstraction. The most interesting thing about it was that he could not make up his mind which end was up. Dawson's paintings have come into vogue since his death in 1967, and although he was once unknown, he is now looked upon as one of the fathers of abstract art.

CHAPTER VIII
ALTERATIONS TO THE CLUBHOUSE

 The first alterations to the new clubhouse were made in 1959. Glen Beach, an architect from Saginaw, came to Ludington to design the new Community Church and was prevailed upon to draw up plans for the remodeling of our clubhouse. Bids were requested for the construction of the project, and two were received for $100,000 and $120,000. The club officials felt this was more than we could afford. Another contractor, Bob Shaw, who was also a member of the club, then offered to do the work for $71,000. The ballroom was enlarged and the porches were made a part of the main room when intervening walls were removed and the floors were raised to the level of the ballroom floor. The bar area was improved and extensively enlarged. The women's locker room was moved from the second floor to the area south of and adjacent to the men's locker room on the main floor, and the men's locker room was enlarged to its present size.

 An apple orchard north of the clubhouse and near the then ninth green was a hindrance to the renovations, and Jack Rasmussen as club president mentioned the fact to his boss, Tom Atkinson, who took it upon himself to have all the trees cut down. As always when trees are removed there was a storm of protest and as a result of this criticism Rasmussen resigned as president of the club. His resignation was not accepted by the board of directors, however, and he continued on as president for a two year period.

Jack Rasmussen club president 1959-1960. (Courtesy of Russ Miller Studios)

A maintenance building was constructed. The parking lot was enlarged and moved from the north side of the clubhouse to its present position east, south and west of the clubhouse and a new practice green was built in the area of the previous parking lot.

Woodrow Wilson once said that the most certain way to make an enemy was to change something. But the storm of protest over these alterations soon dissipated.

A yearly $25 assessment was instituted to pay for these alterations and for the increase in the mortgage that resulted. In 1959 Jack Rasmussen and Herman Yoder, acting as club officials, created a Lincoln Hills Country Club Annex as a further fund-raising effort to help finance the improvements. The annex was a second housing subdivision involving the land adjacent to and south of Golfwood Road. Each member of the club was asked to pay $1,000 or buy one of the new lots. Kim Berger remembers that there were 52 active club members at that time.

Additions were made in the area of the pro shop, professional's office, and lounge in 1965 and 1976, and in 1989 the house committee and the board of directors of Lincoln Hills undertook a second major renovation of the clubhouse. Although minor improvements had been made during the years, this was the first major effort attempted in 30 years. It was felt that it was time to correct some of the effects of aging and wear and tear as well as to improve other aspects of the clubhouse. The total cost of these improvements was predicted to be $225,000.

It was proposed that the board of directors be allowed to renegotiate the club mortgage at the bank which then amounted to $15,850 to $175,000, and that the special assessment already in place to amortize the mortgage be continued and increased by $15 to a total of $40.

The improvements and their proposed cost consisted of:
- A new sign at the main entrance to the club - $3,825
- Oak sign at main entrance to clubhouse - $350
- New awning - $4,850
- Exterior painting - $2,000
- Doors at main entrance and east of the main dining room - $6,135
- New spike-resistant carpet throughout clubhouse - $40,000
- New blinds and draperies in the main dining room - $4,500
- Interior painting - $10,000 and wallpaper - $5,800
- New lighting in dining room, hall, and lounge - $2,500
- New furniture for bar, small dining room and main dining room - $28,000
- Reconstruction of main bar and dining room bar - $20,000
- Ladies' locker room improvements - $6,000
- New ladies' lockers - $7,200
- New kitchen oven - $6,000
- New kitchen freezer - $3,000
- Air conditioning - $30,000 to $40,000
- Contractor - $30,000 and design - $4,500..

As always there was some opposition to the scope and the cost of these improvements. But in the end the proposal for these clubhouse improvements was carried, the increase in special assessment was approved and the clubhouse décor was substantially improved.

We can be proud of our clubhouse. Both the dining room and the bar are attractive and are large enough for our needs. It is a place where we can entertain guests with pride. I have been in the clubhouses of many of the great and famous clubs around the world, and our clubhouse ranks well with them. At Royal Troon in Scotland the benches in the locker room had deep indentations

THE HISTORY OF LINCOLN HILLS GOLF CLUB: One Man's Perspective

in them worn by generations of Scottish buttocks. At Muirfield in Scotland the shower gave out a trickle of water over me as I stood on a wooden lattice above the drain. At Palmetto, a great old course in Aiken, South Carolina the only tap in the sink of the men's locker room was cold and it was attached to a pipe that swayed as the faucet was turned on and off!

In recent years efforts have been made to beautify both the clubhouse area and the course in general. A member, Ralph Johnson, and his brother were involved in early beautification efforts. Lorraine Abrahamson took over these duties and landscaped the rock garden, fountain and pool in front of the clubhouse. She continued these efforts for about ten years with the help of a work bee crew of club members who gathered each spring for clean-up and plantings.

Sharon Tushek joined the greens crew in 1995. She planted flower beds near several of the tees and took over the beautification of the premises. The club sent her to the West Shore Community College where she became a Master Gardener and later an Advanced Master Gardener. Volunteers from among the female members of the club continue to assist her with planting each spring. Sharon always has a happy look whether she is pulling weeds or driving a gang-mower. I told her that it is almost indecent for anyone to enjoy her job that much.

Mrs. Schmock cooked for club dinners. At one time, committee members served as waiters. Most of us were happy to participate. But one member who had emigrated from Northern Europe refused, saying that he had not joined the club to wait on tables. I recall serving at one club dinner where roast beef was the entrée of the meal. I was amused at having the same plate of roast beef refused by one party as being too rare and by the next one as too well-done.

As the years went by the kitchen facilities were improved on at least two occasions. We had a succession of cooks or chefs and eventually a food manager. Chefs had a tendency to become temperamental and disgruntled after a few years, and a succession of food preparers played "Musical Chairs" between Lincoln Hills, the Elk's Club, and various area restaurants.

Some of the names of these cooks or chefs were Mrs. John McCumber, Eddie Haekel, Doris Lokovich, Michael Boyd, and Tom and Sally Teague. Some of them cooked largely for special events. Eventually Friday night dinners were served and shrimp and chicken baskets were available on other evenings.

In 1995 Ann Levandoski, who has now become Ann Bird, took over as food manager, moving from Lakeside Links. Ann made Friday night buffets a special treat. She also offered a limited but varied menu and each weekday night she featured a special such as corned beef and cabbage, roast turkey and dressing, or spaghetti. It is very unusual for a golf club dining room to make a profit, and the dining room of the club to which we belong in South Carolina had losses in the neighborhood of $250,000 to $450,000 for many consecutive years before instituting a club minimum. Still, Ann's dining room has annually shown a profit of around $50,000 and the bar a similar amount for most of the years that she has been employed here. There has been widespread approval of the quality of both the food and the service under her direction.

The dining room has never needed to require a minimum of expenditure as so many clubs have. It has been particularly well supported by the Epworth contingent, which has seen the advantage of having an attractive, well-run dining experience so close to its door. The club has many social members who do not play golf but enjoy the dining opportunities and the parties.

CHAPTER IX
GOLF COURSE ALTERATIONS

All of the holes on the Lincoln Hills Golf Club have been modified, many of them more than once. In order to make the description of these modifications less confusing, we will list the old hole number as the course existed between 1931 and 2000 first in italics followed by the new number in parentheses if the hole still exists.

When the clubhouse was moved to its present site in 1931 and a parking lot was installed to the north of the clubhouse, what then became the first hole was markedly shortened as the tee was moved northward from the edge of the bank overlooking the Lincoln River and the L&N tracks in order to make space for the new building. The original second hole was a par 3 of 187 yards with the tee located just south of the woods at the end of the present driving range. One of the early alterations of the course in the early 1950s involved moving the first green north some 100 yards to its present site where it now functions as the eighth green. This made for a longer par 4 hole, but it now offered an undesirably blind second shot. Later the hill which blocked the view of the green was removed and the hole was thus substantially improved.

Aerial view of Lincoln Hills golf course. (Courtesy of Russ Miller Studios)

The original par 3 second hole was made into a dogleg par 4 as the tee was moved back beside the new first green. It made for an interesting uphill tee shot which had to skirt or carry the woods on the left in order for a long drive to remain in the fairway. The hole's chief problem was that the tee shot was blind. A tall mirror was installed on the tee to make the shot less hazardous for the players ahead. Both these holes were lost to the expanded driving range in 2000.

The 10th [1] tee was moved back from its position where the ladies' tee still remains, to near its present location, making the previously straight hole longer and a slight dogleg to the right. The 9th [18] green was moved to its present position from an area in an apple orchard opposite the old 10th [1] tee. The 11th [2] tee was also moved well back from its former position behind and to the north of the 8th [17] green. This made it a longer hole which dog-legged left. The 17th [8] tee was also moved back. All these changes made longer more difficult holes and the change on the 2nd increased the course par to 70. At the same time the 18th [9] green was relocated to the west to make it safer from stray tee shots coming from the new 10th [1] tee.

Through the years many other modifications were made. In 1983 an agreement was made with Epworth to exchange four pieces of property. The exchange made Lincoln Lake and the Lincoln River the natural boundary between the two properties. It gave Epworth title to an area west of the golf course for use as a drain field. And it gave Lincoln Hills title to the area on which were located the maintenance building and the new tee on the 3rd [10], which lengthened that hole. The 4th [13] tee was also moved back, substantially lengthening that hole. The tee on the 6th [15] was enlarged and moved to the south and the tees on the 12th [3], 13th [4], 14th [5], 15th [6] and 16th [7] were all enlarged and moved back.

All of the greens have been enlarged, moved, or altered in their slope, some of them more than once. I will mention a few of the changes which were most significant. The 6th [15] green was originally a bowl with the lowest point lying in the middle of the green. When the green was rebuilt, the bowl effect was completely removed. The 7th [16] green was narrow from front to back and elevated. The present green is several times the size of the old green and is much easier to approach. The 11th [2] green was narrow and sharply tilted up from front to back. The new green is much larger, flatter and it is protected by new bunkers.

The original 13th [4] green was in a depression thirty yards or so to the west of its present position. The new mounded green was built by Eddie Ackersville's crew in the late 1960s. The green of the 14th [5] was steeply slanting down from back to front. As you see your ball drifting down off the front of the green these days, you may be frustrated, but it was worse before its alteration, and the steep slope involved the entire green.

Crucial bunkers have been added or modified on several holes, most notably on the 3rd [10], both along the fairway and at the green, the 6th [15], 7th [16], in the rough to the right of the 9th [18], and on several of the holes on what is now the front nine.

A major improvement in the course has been achieved by the long term judicious planting of trees, altering the entire character of the course from a classic links style, in the tradition of the famous Scottish courses, to that of a parkland setting. All the tree plantings were planned by a tree committee, and their variety and location were carefully and strategically selected. Most of the planted trees come into play, and almost any stray shot will result in the ball lying near, under or behind a tree. The trees not only add to the difficulty and the strategic play of the course, but they add to the beauty of it as well.

One of the improvements made in the 1950s was the removal of several large low-spreading junipers which were situated in the rough to the left of the 4th [13], over the hill to the right of the 7th [16] and in front of the tee on the 17th [8]. These were ugly and impossible to play from. Everyone was delighted to see them go.

After the course was improved by the application of water to the fairways there were yearly minor changes made to the course to make it more playable. One area of dissatisfaction was the 8th [17]. This par three hole rose steeply from the tee up a bank commonly known as "Cardiac Hill" to a flat, rather narrow green. There were no bunkers, and although the pin was visible from below, it was an essentially blind shot to a green without definition. The chief complaint was that many good shots which landed on the green rolled over it into unfavorable lies. To stay on the green the ball had to either bounce up the hill or light near the front edge of the green. There was also dissatisfaction with the 17th [8], which was a long par 4. The long second shot offered no clear view of the putting surface.

One of the major concerns of the club officials was the driving range. It was in its present location, but it was situated between the old first and second fairways and was much narrower than it is now. It had teeing mats instead of grass, and there was limited teeing space. What was much worse was that sliced shots from the range often entered the first fairway while hooks sometimes went into the second fairway. A hooked shot from either the first or second tee usually ended up on the range. This was invariably followed by a prolonged "Easter Egg Hunt" as the player tried to identify his ball among the thousands of practice balls lying on the range. There was potential for injury to players on these holes, and the possibility of a resulting law suit was a continual concern.

At times golfers on the range had to stop their practicing and wait until players on the course got out of their way. Occasionally they didn't wait.

No easy solution could be found for this problem. The installation of high fences along the range was suggested but this measure was considered impractical and defacing. It was suggested that the range be placed in the area south of the entrance drive near the tennis courts, but the distance from the clubhouse made this location unacceptable.

The decision was made to go outside the club to get professional advice on future course alterations for the first time in the history of the club. Before this time, all alterations had been planned by the greens committee and carried out by our own greens crew. The firm of Bruce and Jerry Matthews from the Grand Haven Golf Club was engaged. The Matthews duo inspected the course thoroughly and drew up a long range plan for alterations and improvements. This was presented to the club on July 27, 1984.

The suggestions made by the Matthews team were extensive. According to their estimates, full implementation of the changes would cost the club $260,494, and would entail some disruption of play.

The most important feature of the Matthews plan was to enlarge the driving range by doing away with the old first and second holes. New holes to replace these would be a 390 yard par four hole running from east to west, north of and adjacent to and parallel to the present 13th hole, and a 480 yard dogleg par 5 north of the other new hole with the green to be located near the present 14th tee. It was suggested that a pond be constructed in front of the present 15th green. The present 17th hole was to be extensively remodeled. New greens were planned for what are now the 3rd, 4th, 6th, and 16th. Many hills were to be removed or modified. The tee on what is now the 9th was to be moved back and to the west making the hole longer and a sharper dogleg right.

The club greens keeper at the time, Brian Hamilton, was against removing the hills, saying that these hills were a part of the course's charm. Many of us hated to lose the first two holes, both of which had their supporters. Many of us thought that the disruption of play and the debt which would be incurred by the project were too high a price for us to pay. So these plans were put on the back burner.

In the end only two holes were modified by the Matthews firm in 1986. The remodeling of what is now the 17th hole was extensive and controversial. In spite of lowering the hill, the green was still invisible from the tee. The mounds which were built around the hole, while common on modern courses, were not in keeping with the rest of our old style course. The turf on the green was very slow to mature, leading to some discussion as to whether we should do the entire green over again, but cooler heads prevailed, and with time and care the green became acceptable. There was a wide difference of opinion over whether this venture had been a success. The cost for this project was estimated at $13,950. The other modification undertaken by Matthews was the rebuilding of the old green on what is now the 8th hole at a cost of $15,185. Since this green has been completely removed by the renovations of 2000, it is not worth discussing here.

CHAPTER X
EMPLOYEES OF THE CLUB

We could find little information about the early employees of the club. We know that Harry Webster, the pro at Epworth, was involved in some capacity with Lincoln Hills during the early years. A. W. Church, in an article about Lincoln Hills which was published in the Ludington Daily News in July of 1931, mentioned that their pro at the time, Larry Weichman, had set the course record of 63. This is the only other mention that we could find of a Lincoln Hills professional before 1948. Some of the old caddies described Howard Jury as being a pro and giving golf lessons, but Howard's son Chuck, a long-time member, is definite that his father was not a professional although he was a scratch golfer.

Laborers were employed to lay the pipes, to sow the original grass seed, and occasionally mow the fairways and greens by hand. Dick Meissner says that his uncle Alden Love, a mighty man, was the greens-keeper in the mid-thirties. He mowed all the greens with a hand mower which he transported from green to green in a wheelbarrow. The first mention in the club log of a greens-keeper is in the minutes of 1948, when George West was hired for $1,500 for the season to be a professional and greens-keeper with the emphasis on the greens-keeping part of the job. The next year West was offered $2,000 to do the same job. Whether he accepted this offer is unclear.

Russell Collins was noted earlier to have offered to plant trees on the course for $2.50 per tree. He became a full-time employee, and the club records show that in 1942 with the club still wallowing in the Depression years, Collins was paid 65 cents an hour and his laborers were paid 50 cents an hour. In 1950 Collins was empowered to collect green fees from players who were playing but were not members of the club. In 1952 it is noted that Collins was being paid $1.25 per hour and his laborers $1. Collins was himself a laborer without any educational advantages, but he continued to serve as keeper of the greens for many years. In the autumn of 1952 it was noted that Russell Collins was threatening to go to Muskegon to work. He was then paid a $150 bonus and was guaranteed at least $100 per week for the 24 weeks of the next golf season.

Prior to the 1960 season, Lloyd Rathbun was hired as greens-keeper and he continued in this position until 1967 when Eddie Ackersville was hired to oversee the course and its laborers. Eddie had owned a hardware store on Ludington Avenue which had just been sold. Although he had spent his life working with hardware, he too had no special training in turf or greens management. Eddie continued working for the club for several years managing the laboring crew which often consisted of one or two regulars and a couple of college students who worked on the course during their summer vacation.

The first trained greens-keeper at Lincoln Hills was Rick Grunch who was hired in 1972. He began a succession of mostly college-trained turf experts, who worked at the club for a few years before being replaced. Each did a better job of improving the course than his predecessor. The men who succeeded Rick Grunch were David Timms who was hired in 1977, John McCumber, Brian Hamilton, Maynard Garner, and presently Dennis Cook, who was hired in 2000. Dennis was at the top of his class in turf management at Michigan State University. At present Dennis has a crew of nine working full-time on the course.

In 1950 Walter Paukstis, the brother of Dr. Charles Paukstis, a Ludington physician and club member, was hired to look after the clubhouse. He was responsible for the clubhouse condition, for bar-tending, and for collecting fees. He was paid $110 per week, with free lodging in two rooms and a bath on the second floor of the clubhouse. A liquor license was obtained and over the next three years James Eller, Walter Paukstis again, and Clarence Hannig fulfilled the clubhouse duties with much the same remuneration arrangement.

Dr. Charles Paukstis was club president from 1951 to 1952. (Courtesy of Chuck and Glenna Paukstis).

In 1954 Don Kooyers from Muskegon was hired to become both club manager and professional. Mr. Kooyers' skills as a golf professional were limited, but he did give lessons. There is a notation in the minutes that Kooyers protested Hal Madden, who was a high school coach and teacher, giving golf lessons to high school students. This was resolved in Madden's favor as long as he did not charge for the service.

Harold Madden was club president in 1976. (Courtesy of Russ Miller Studios)

The most interesting employee to work as a professional at Lincoln Hills was Bill Black, who was hired in 1960. Bill was a middle-aged pro who had spent his life playing and working at golf in Florida. He had played in tour events against famous golfers like Gene Sarazen and Walter Hagen, and was an exceptional golfer and a great teacher. I believe that this was his first experience as a club pro this far north. I recall taking a lesson from Bill on May 12th. I was active during the lesson and was quite comfortable, but Bill was wearing a long overcoat and was shaking all over with the cold.

Bill Black was not only exceptionally talented, he was also exceptionally thin-skinned. Everything bothered him. When Bill first arrived, a reception was held for him. Jack Shillinger, who owned a gift shop downtown, was a joker, practical and otherwise. Jack also had a hoarse stage whisper which could be heard a block away. When Jack walked into the reception, he swaggered up to Bill, stuck out his hand and said, "I'm Jack Shillinger, if you need any help with your golf game, feel free to call on me". Bill Black's sense of humor was non-existent and he took instant umbrage.

At our first stag, Bill showed slides of famous people whom he had met. He had played golf with some of them and had given lessons to others. Some of the slides were underexposed and not of the best quality. Jack Shillinger leaned over to me and said in his stage whisper, "the first thing we've got to do is chip in and buy this SOB a light-meter". That and a few other remarks did not sit well with Bill Black. Bill played golf with my foursome once. Gerald Ponko Sr. was my regular golfing companion, and we needled each other constantly in a friendly way. By the time we reached the ninth hole, Bill had had enough. He said, "I can't stand this!" and walked off the course.

Bill's wife worked in the clubhouse, and she didn't get along with the ladies of the club at all. By the Fourth of July, Bill had had a bellyful. Between freezing, having an unhappy wife, and having his feeling bruised, he couldn't wait to get out of Ludington. We regretted losing him because he knew more about golf than anyone I ever met.

In 1958 Harry Eastman took over as manager of the club, and he held that position for the next 16 years. Harry had owned the sports shop on Ludington Avenue, later run by Len Edmondson. Harry was a polished and diplomatic man and was popular with the clientele. He was influential enough and carried himself with so much aplomb that many casual golfers thought that Harry owned the club. Harry continued as manager until his nephew Byron Higgins, a United States Navy commander, retired from the service and took over the position in 1974. Byron ran the club until 1994, when his duties were assumed by Tom Baldwin who had come to Lincoln Hills as a professional in 1987.

Harold King was the club secretary at its inception in 1921, and he continued in that capacity for a good many years. He was followed by Len Nielsen who became the club secretary and also functioned as the business manager of the club until his retirement in 1987.

CHAPTER XI
THE BY-LAWS AND THE BOARD OF DIRECTORS

The by-laws of the club provided for nine directors to be elected by the active members of the club on an annual basis. The terms were for three years, staggered so that six board members were retained each year while three were subject to election. The president and other officials were elected from and by the board. Board members were limited to two consecutive terms of three years each.

The first elected board of directors consisted of M. B. Danaher, one of the early lumbermen; Arthur Anderson, the head of the great accounting firm; H. L. Haskell, founder of the Haskell Boat Company and inventor of an industrial material called Haskelite; A. H. Cantrell; W. L. Hammond; T. L. Gatke, the course designer from Epworth; and W. T. Culver.

W. T. Culver was elected president of the club. He gave way in 1923 to A. W. Church as president and Church continued in that capacity through 1934. Another influential club member was Turk Matthews who was a long-time board member, adviser and club president.

The original by-laws allowed active members to cast three votes for any of the candidates for the board. They could split the votes among the candidates or cast all three votes for one candidate. This method of voting made it possible for a small number of members with an agenda, or even one member with a number of absentee ballots in his hand, to railroad a preferred member through the election process each year. That man or group of men could always control a third of the board.

For many years Harry Eastman was the club manager. Like most managers and CEOs who had to answer to a board of directors, Harry saw the desirability of not only pleasing his board, but of making sure that those directors who were elected were people he could count on for support. Since the annual meetings and elections occurred in the fall after most Epworth members had left for the winter, Harry kept on friendly terms with these people and easily prevailed upon most of them to give him their proxies. With the three-vote-for-one rule and the proxies at hand, Harry could make sure that the board was always a friendly one toward him.

Many of us considered that this method of election was unfair and counterproductive to the democratic process. Talking did little good, but when Hal Madden became a board member, he introduced an amendment to the by-laws eliminating multiple votes for any one candidate.

On one occasion a club member was nominated to run for the board of directors who did not meet the approval of the sitting board. His application was rejected and the by-laws were amended to create a nominating committee made up of three past presidents of the board and chosen by the sitting president. This committee served to screen further nominees as to suitability of background, ability, and purpose. There was opposition to this amendment which was seen by some members as a rejection of the democratic process and which encouraged elitism or cronyism. When the by-laws were revised in 2002 this nominating committee was deleted. Thereafter any member who can get 20 supporters on a petition can have his name on the ballot and run for the board.

The name of the club after 85 years remains Lincoln Hills Golf Club rather than Lincoln Hills Country Club. There has been a difference of opinion among the club members as to the goals of the club. A part of the membership is for diversification with the emphasis on such pursuits as tennis, swimming, and clubhouse activities. The other group insists that the primary purpose of the club is golf, that the chief earner of revenues is golf, and that most of the dues and green fees be put back into the golf course in the form of improvements to the course and for its upkeep.

Whenever clubhouse improvements were suggested, there was opposition from the golf course enthusiasts. In 1974, a group of tennis-playing members got together and collected donations of $1,000 from each interested member to build tennis courts on the land south of the entrance road. The donation actually was treated as a loan and the interest on the loan replaced dues for the tennis facility. Apparently the board of directors approved the project, but it was not brought to a vote of the membership.

Bob Erickson from the Carrom Company and later a founder of Merdel Manufacturing Co. was in direct opposition not only to this undertaking but especially to the manner in which it was approved. He says that he asked a member of the board why the project was not brought to a member vote. The answer was that in this man's opinion the majority of the members would not have approved it.

Robert Erickson was club president in 1970. (Courtesy of Russ Miller Studios)

The by-laws of the club were amended at that time in an attempt to make it illegal for the board to spend money for projects other than golf without membership approval. But two years later the board approved an expenditure of $13,000 to erect toilets at the site of the tennis courts. Erickson again objected, not to the toilets themselves, but to the board taking the authority to approve the project without securing membership approval. A legal opinion was sought at this time. It was a waffling sort of opinion, but the tenor of it was that the amendment involved was not clearly enough written to make the project illegal.

The Lincoln Hills board, like the functioning boards of many other entities, seems to have sometimes made decisions which it felt was for the betterment of the club without securing membership approval. When such situations occurred, the board acted either because it felt that securing membership approval was too cumbersome and time-consuming or because it was doubtful of securing a vote of approval while at the same time being certain of the worthiness of its cause. Whenever the board's enthusiasm for its cause exceeded its legal right to act, Bob Erickson, as gadfly, was there to protest and object.

CHAPTER XII
THE COURSE RENOVATION OF 2000

By 1998 the balance of power in the club had changed. The oldsters who remembered the Great Depression and the time of the overwhelming Lincoln Hills' debt were in the minority and fading rapidly. Their place had been taken by younger members who had no memory of the Depression or of hard times, who had unlimited confidence in the future, and who in their own personal lives lived comfortably with mortgages, car payments, credit card debt, and buying their household appliances and toys on time.

The Great Depression was not a pleasant thing to go through, but it taught my generation a number of lessons that we never forgot. We learned that good times don't last forever, and that it is prudent to save for a rainy day. It taught us that we could get along without things that we wanted and yet we could still be happy. And we learned to postpone doing things and buying things until we could afford them. It taught us that if we postponed acquiring something until we could afford it, we appreciated and valued it more and took better care of it. We learned fiscal responsibility.

My generation had continued its conservative monetary philosophy for 43 years, while husbanding the Lincoln Hills Golf Club through some harrowing times, arranging for the buyout from the bond-holders and making constant course improvements a little at a time in order to avoid subjecting the club to any repetition of its former overwhelming debt. We did not implement the renovation plan proposed by the Matthews firm in 1984, because we thought that the debt which would be incurred and the disturbance of play were too high a price to pay for what was primarily an improved driving range.

The older members of the club had seen their dues rise from $75 to more than fifteen hundred dollars and they had experienced several long-term assessments. Many of them were on fixed incomes and because of continual inflation were afraid that they might eventually run out of money. Some of them now played only the occasional golf game, and when they divided their dues by the number of rounds played, they came up with some startling numbers.

So the stage was set for a big generation-gap difference of opinion between the "Stay Out of Debt" members and the "I Want it All and I Want it Now" group. These diverse attitudes would cause a number of resignations, some hard feelings, and would put the club's financial status in jeopardy.

The younger members became enthusiastic about revising and lengthening the golf course, raising its par to 72, and enlarging and improving the driving range. They hired the firm of Earth Partnership Inc. of Minneapolis, Minnesota as golf course consultants. Mark Mitchell was their representative. Mitchell's suggestions were in many ways similar to those of the Matthews firm.

Here we revert to the problems involved with the building of the railroad spur to the Piney Ridge area, first mentioned in the chapter on Epworth Heights' history. The following has been researched by Cassius Street and is related mostly in his own words.

In 1916, five 50 foot-wide strips of land were deeded at the cost of one dollar to the L&N Railroad by the Epworth Assembly and by W. L. Hammond and Charles Hagerman representing the Stearns interests in the land which later became Lincoln Hills Golf Club. The parcels were to be used "for railroad purposes only" and the deeds were "subject to termination by a condition subsequent". This condition was that if the property was not used for railroad purposes for more than a year, the property would revert back to its grantors.

Before the one year period of non-use had expired, the Michigan legislature under heavy pressure from the powerful railroad lobby passed a law which said that if a grantor of land to a railroad, subject to reversion under the condition of non-use, did not record a Notice of Intent to Rely on Such Reverter within one year of the effective date of this law, the Reverter Clause was extinguished and the railroad would own the strip outright. There was no public disclosure to this law, and it was so little known that no

Notices of Intent were ever published in the 83 Michigan counties despite the fact that there were hundreds and perhaps thousands of such deeds recorded throughout Michigan. The same laws were passed nationally. This law was later judged by many to be unfair and was passed through the legislature in an underhanded and secretive way.

Epworth believed that the law which voided the Reverter Clause was unconstitutional [i.e. the taking of private property from individuals without compensation] and some time after the Sargent Sand Co. had ceased its operations in 1982 Epworth barred the railroad from access to property on their land. The railroad sued. Epworth asked Lincoln Hills to join them in their suit which if successful would mean that all five strips conveyed to the railroad by Epworth and Lincoln Hills property owners would revert to them. Lincoln Hills refused on the basis that if Epworth was successful in their suit, Lincoln Hills would get its property back without its participation. In 1992 the railroads won the suit and thus owned the strips in fee simple.

Five years later, in 1997, the Epworth League bought all of the L&N right-of-way from M-116 to the Ludington city limits. The property recovered was 13,523 feet or approximately 2.6 miles. They again asked Lincoln Hills to join with them in the purchase, proportionately to the amount of land recovered by each party. Epworth paid $130,000 to recover this strip. To Epworth's disappointment, Lincoln Hills again refused, saying that the land was not of any interest or use to them. Hindsight is better than foresight, but in retrospect these refusals were critical errors by the Lincoln Hills board which caused a hostile reaction on Epworth's part and haunted Lincoln Hills in its plans for the use of this land in later years.

Epworth donated the recovered area through Cartier Park to the City of Ludington, paved the part in Epworth as a walking trail, paved and held the area through Lincoln Hills property as a walking trail and as a way of keeping Lincoln Hills from using its land to the south of the entrance road for interests not acceptable to Epworth.

The golf course renovation Plan A, proposed by Mark Mitchell, involved building three new holes on the vacant land south of the entrance road. Epworth Heights owned the 50 foot wide strip of land which it had purchased from the Sargent Sand Co. and which passed through the middle of this area. The promoters of the project assured the membership that Epworth would be willing to grant an easement for the use of this land or would offer it for sale to Lincoln Hills. This was assumed despite repeated warnings from some Epworth members indicating that their board had no such intent.

Displays were posted in the Lincoln Hills clubhouse explaining the project and assuring the membership that the project could be completed by the disposition of the club contingency fund without incurring any further debt. Many of us felt that this was impossible, and we were apprehensive that the spending of this fund would leave the club unable to meet its future obligations. A vote was taken by the membership asking for approval of the project, and it was passed. However the Epworth board flatly refused to give any kind of easement or to offer the property in question for sale.

After this rebuff, the board of directors went to "Plan B" which involved opening two new holes north and west of the third green in the general area that the Matthews firm had chosen for expansion. The supporters of this plan went ahead with it without asking for further approval by the membership. Some senior members objected to the scope and expense of these plans, but the younger members were impatient with the caution of their seniors, whose objections were ignored or sometimes refuted in unpleasant ways. One older member was told, "We don't care about you old guys or whether you resign from the club!" Another was told, "Why should you worry about a ten year assessment? You're going to be dead anyway!"

The alterations were undertaken in 1998. They were extensive and were continued over a two year period and were completed in the year 2000 and involved some continual disruption of play. The first two holes were abandoned and incorporated into the driving range. The two new holes were built north and west of the present 10th green. This was in the dune area. At first the DNR objected to the environmental impact of these holes, but Nordlund and Associates were hired to survey the area and determined that the holes could be built while preserving the pristine environmentally sensitive areas. The former 18th hole was drastically altered, many new tees were built and others were enlarged, and a portion of the hill in front of the present 13th tee was removed eliminating the blind tee shot. The nines were reversed. The contingency fund of $231,465 was emptied; the mortgage was increased to $110,660.16.

In December 1999 the board came up with a plan to make further improvements to Lincoln Hills. The projects involved were:

> Cart path improvements - $139,000
> Kitchen upgrade - $49,000
> Bar cooler replacement - $8,000
> Maintenance/greens building - $115,000
> Asphalt parking area around maintenance building - $25,000
> Men's locker room upgrade - $14,000

The total of $350,000 was to be paid for by a ten year assessment of $100 a year or a one year $700 assessment.

There was a storm of protest over the scope and expense of this project, coming on the heels of the previous club indebtedness from the golf course alterations, and at Bob Erickson's insistence a meeting of the club members was called. Most of the members of the board of directors boycotted the meeting, but one member presided and agreed to hear the complaints, although he said that it was already "a done deal". As a result of the complaints, the maintenance building and the asphalt parking lot were postponed and the cart path project was cut back. The assessment was reduced to $60 a year for ten years.

The fallout of these two major projects having been put through so close together in time will be discussed in the chapter on membership.

CHAPTER XIII
MEMBERSHIP

In the beginning there were 71 members of Lincoln Hills. These were the founding fathers of the club. About half of them were from Epworth, and most of these initial members were also members of the Ludington Country Club. The Ludington members were mostly prominent citizens, businessmen, doctors or lawyers. Each of the founding members took out a $100 bond to get the club off to a good start.

In 1925 the membership of the club made significant loans to the club to keep it going. R. L. Stearns, M. B. Danaher, O. A. Starke, and W. A. Church each contributed $2,000 and fourteen others contributed from $150 to $500. The $2,000 contribution was equivalent to at least $40,000 in today's currency and it indicates the degree of devotion that these members displayed toward making the club a success.

The club was visited by hard times as the Great Depression hit the country in 1929. It is clear that Ludington was very slow to recover from the Depression as the membership numbers continued to dwindle.

> In 1931 there were 105 total members, some being only golf or social members.
> In 1936 there were 86 total members.
> In 1939 there were 51 active members.
> In 1940 there were 47 active members.
> In 1941 there were 43 active members and 24 greens fee members.
> In 1946 there were only 38 active members.

The lowest membership number on record was 25 and annual dues at that time were cut from $95 to $50. That means that the total amount realized in that year from dues was $1,250, and except for the few greens fees, this was all the money available to pay the club's obligations. The club president, A. W. Church, personally cosigned for bank loans to keep the course viable. Contrast that $1,250 with the recent club's annual budget of nearly one million dollars.

By 1948 the active membership had increased to 58. As the economy improved and as television coverage of golf brought heroes like Arnold Palmer and Jack Nicklaus to viewers' attention, more people started to play golf everywhere. As the Lincoln Hills course improved and general interest in the game increased the membership burgeoned.

In 1976 membership was limited to 400 and there was a waiting list. In 1979 the membership limit was increased to 450. Later the bylaws were changed to allow 500 members. This quota was eventually filled and there was still a waiting list of 50. In 1991 it was noted that all 500 memberships were filled and there were also 175 social members. During the summer months, play was so heavy that it was difficult to find an empty spot on the course even late in the afternoon. As late as 1998 the active membership was listed as 501.

For many years Lincoln Hills was the only choice if people wanted to play golf in Mason County. To the north Manistee Country Club was the closest alternative. To play a quality course in that direction one had to travel to Crystal Downs north of Crystal Lake. Even that course was not in top condition until a fairway watering system was installed around 1970.

To the south there were originally nine holes at Hart Golf Club, but that facility folded long ago. There was a quirky nine holes at Oceana Country Club north of Shelby that was later increased to 18 holes. White Lake Country Club was available for a while until it became private. Muskegon Country Club was private. Pontaluna Golf Club south of Muskegon was open for golf, but to play a really good course in that direction one had to travel to Grand Haven. To the east there was no golf course at all until one got to Clare, Big Rapids, or Cadillac.

This changed when the Ludington Hills course was opened in 1975 as nine holes, then 18, and now 27. Its name has been changed to Lakeside Links, and its conditioning and clubhouse have been substantially improved. More recently the Colonial Golf Club opened 27 holes in Hart, and the Hemlock Golf Club was built on Decker Road in Ludington. The latter is a difficult and highly rated course. Play on all three of these courses is competitively priced.

Manistee National has two new championship courses which have been built on US 31 south of Manistee. Other courses in the area include Grandview, The Thoroughbred, Golden Sands, and Benona Shores. Marquette Trails has opened a course at Big Star Lake near Baldwin.

Lincoln Hills has lost members to each of the area's courses. In the previous chapter in which we described the extensive golf course alterations begun in 1998 followed immediately by the major indebtedness incurred by the new projects in 1999, we noted the dissatisfaction of some senior members, many of whom then resigned from the club.

Within a period of two years, the club found itself with its active membership reduced from the previous 500 with a waiting list down to the middle 300s. Income from membership and assessments was diminished by nearly a third and the club was in a financial bind. With reduced revenue, it now had difficulty covering its usual expenses as well as paying interest and principal on the new mortgage. It was a Catch 22 situation. If the club increased its dues, more members might drop out. This sudden membership loss was ascribed to normal attrition of the aging membership, but it was more than that.

In a way the situation in which the club found itself was similar to that of the family which has extended itself in buying things on time, but is able to meet its obligations as long as both husband and wife are healthy and employed. But when one of them gets sick or loses his or her job, the house, the car, the boat, and all the household appliances are in danger of being repossessed.

The younger board members had miscalculated in three ways. They had shown a lack of appreciation of the value of the membership dues of the older members. They also had shown a lack of understanding of what the older members would stand for in accepting debt, assessments, and dues increases. Finally they failed to realize that unhappy members were no longer a captive group, but had many other golfing options. To be fair, the club would have come through both expensive projects unscathed if so many members had not resigned.

With the reduced membership, it was pleasant for the remaining players to be able to access the golf course at almost any hour and to play without either undue pressure or delay, but to continue on in the present country club style with a pro, a food manager, a dinning room, and a full golf course maintenance crew, more revenue would be necessary. The board of directors cast about for ways of increasing both income and membership. Some revenue was generated by granting the right to do seismic testing for oil in the area, but no oil wells were drilled and only about $20,000 was raised in 2002 by those activities.

In its concern, the board contacted the contractor Cal Prins and plans were drawn up to build 160 condominiums in the area south of the entrance road. Profits in the millions from the proposed undertaking were predicted for the club. Perhaps these optimistic predictions were pie in the sky. At any rate, Epworth continued to refuse to grant access to the land involved, refused to sell the L&N strip, and refused to make a trade of the L&N strip for a more valuable strip along the river. As a result the entire condo project was abandoned.

Epworth made offers to purchase the involved property from Lincoln Hills, which the Lincoln Hills board felt were both inadequate and involved too many restrictions. These offers were refused. Hot-heads on both sides were unable to reach any compromise. Lincoln Hills' board members felt that they were unable to obtain a reasonable offer for the property until they had the right of access to the area along the Lincoln River.

In 2004 Lincoln Hills sued Epworth for the right to cross the L&N strip and gain access to their land south of the strip. This suit angered many of the Epworth members and some of them gave up their Lincoln Hills memberships, thus further aggravating the already serious membership crisis. Lincoln Hills eventually won the suit.

The ultimate best use of the land involved in the suit was clearly by Epworth because of its location. After the lawsuit was settled in

Lincoln Hills' favor, Epworth substantially increased its offer for the land, and a committee made up of cooler heads on both sides worked out satisfactory details of the agreement which involved a purchase price of $3,000,000 without restrictions on either side.

In the beginning Lincoln Hills was a non-profit institution. The club lost that tax benefit along the way when the IRS determined that the club derived too much of its revenue from non-member sources. No attempt was made to revive this status until the deal with Epworth was consummated. Now efforts are being made to secure this tax advantage so that the parts of the settlement which will be used to improve the club facilities come to us tax-free.

As I write this, Lincoln Hills is coming into possession of the three million dollars and the interest which the escrow fund has earned in the interim. The present board of directors has made a decision to promote using the majority of these funds to build a new clubhouse and to drastically revamp the watering system of the golf course. They have sold this idea to a membership which was overwhelmingly against using these funds in that manner. Their prime argument was that any unused funds would be heavily taxed and that repairs of the clubhouse would be expensive.

The board viewed this windfall as a once-in-a-lifetime opportunity to renew the facilities. The alternative option, to make only necessary improvements, pay tax on the rest, pay off the mortgage, and invest the remainder, was a once-in-a-lifetime opportunity for financial stability.

There is one thing that we can be certain of, and that is that this club got its "mulligan" when the public-spirited bond-holders settled the overwhelming Lincoln Hills debt in 1955 for ten cents on the dollar and let the club off the hook. Such generosity by its creditors will never be seen again, and we can be certain that if the club fails to meet its financial obligations in the future, it will either become someone else's golf course or a housing development.

Some of us have noted that whenever there is a windfall, vultures are waiting with proposals which are too good to pass up and which relieve the recipient of his funds. The telephone rings off the wall with proposals which seem too good to be true. The board assures us that not all of the funds will be spent on these ventures, and that a contingency fund will remain. Experience tells us that in projects of this magnitude there are always cost overruns, and that even if a builder makes guarantees, circumstances always arise which necessitate extra funding beyond the original plan. Time will tell whether factors like depreciation on the new projects will offset increased taxation and other expenses.

We are in a time of economic turmoil where jobs are going overseas, where there is increased unemployment, hundreds of houses are for sale, mortgages are being foreclosed, businesses and banks are closing, and the J and J Ranch is in bankruptcy. History tells us that in hard times golf is the first thing to go. If club dues continue to rise, it seems certain that many golfers will leave, forcing dues to continue to spiral. The result will be either bankruptcy or an elite membership.

Time will tell whether this ambitious building plan is the making or the breaking of the club.

CHAPTER XIV
TOURNAMENTS AND CHAMPIONS

The first Lincoln Hills Club Championship was held in 1922 the year after the club opened. The winner was J. B. Bussey. There was no champion in 1929, perhaps because of the stock market crash. No championships were held between 1933 and 1942, undoubtedly because of the Depression and the decline in membership to a low of 25.

There have been a variety of winners of the men's club championship throughout the 85 years of the club's existence, and a list of these will be appended to this book. A few of the multiple winners will be discussed in more detail.

By all odds the most significant men's champion was Otto A. Starke Jr. universally known as "Bub" to distinguish him from his father O. A. Starke Sr., one of the founding fathers of the Lincoln Hills Golf Club. Bub was just a young fellow when the club was formed. He became the secretary of the Star Watchcase Company and after his father's death was named the president of the company. He was president of Lincoln Hills in 1938 and 1939.

Otto A. "Bub" Starke Jr. club president 1938-1939. (Courtesy of Russ Miller Studios)

Bub won his first club championship in 1925 and he repeated the feat a total of fifteen times over the next forty years, the last time in 1965. He won the championship five straight years between 1944 and 1948. His record is even more remarkable when one considers that the championship was not held at all for eleven years during Bub's hey-day. His winning this championship in five different decades was a remarkable accomplishment.

I played a few matches against Bub, so I can tell you first hand a little about him and his golf game. He was not a long hitter, but he was accurate. He had a smooth, graceful, fairly-long unhurried swing. He was particularly effective with his niblick, a thin-bladed lofted club which had no flange. In this way it was unlike the present-day wedge. He could slip this blade under the ball and hit his approach shots consistently close to the hole.

Like Ben Hogan and other great golfers, Bub was a somewhat difficult and self-centered man. As a competitor he was relentless, giving no quarter or sympathy to his opponent. As an example, I recall one final club championship match in later years between Bub and Francis "Pierre" LaFond, a much less experienced player. The match was all-square going into the last hole. Bub pushed his tee shot on the 18th to the right into the rough behind some trees, while Pierre's drive was on top of the hill in the fairway short of the green. Bub took an interminable amount of time to play the obvious shot, walking back and forth between his ball and the possible landing spots. After what seemed like ages, he played the obvious shot out to the fairway. By that time Pierre's nerves were frazzled from the waiting. He dumped his pitch shot into a bunker, took two to get it out and lost the match.

Years later Se Ri Pak used the same ploy to win a U.S. Women's Open Championship that it appeared she had lost. She hit her crucial tee shot into a creek and took a ridiculous amount time deciding whether to play the ball or to take a drop and a penalty. Her inexperienced amateur opponent's nerves could not withstand the pressure of the long wait, and she eventually three-putted and lost her advantage.

This is called "gamesmanship". It is a legal but somewhat questionable part of golf, which is a gentleman's game in which a player is discouraged from performing any activity which is distracting or upsetting to his opponent. However, Seve Ballesteros, one of the great golfers of all-time was an expert at this. Among other tactics, he jangled change in his pocket, started walking while his opponent was at the top of his backswing, and demanded that his opponent replace his ball by the cup after his opponent had tapped it in out of turn.

The next significant men's championship winner was Len Edmondson, who won the club tournament four times between 1956 and 1964. Len was a smooth golfer with a nice short game. Like Bub, he was not a long hitter. I played a round once with Len, Ross "Dusty" DesEnfants, and Jack Shillinger. We were on the long hole by the highway which is now sixteen. Dusty hit his tee shot about 275 yards, mine was out about 250, Jack's ball was at 225 and Len's was only around 200. As Len prepared to hit his second shot, Shillinger delivered the following line in his loud hoarse stage whisper, "is he *really* the club champion?"

Len Edmondson was club president 1955-1956. (Courtesy of Russ Miller Studios)

On a cold but snowless January day in 1965, Len called me, asking me to play golf. So Len, Karl Schwaibold, my dog Speedy Gonzales, and I played 18 holes at Lincoln Hills over the frozen turf. We had a really good time, and a picture of us on the course was in the newspaper the next day. That next night Len died suddenly of a heart attack. He had been having anginal chest pains before we played, but didn't mention it to me or to any other doctor.

He apparently wasn't going to give in to the pain, thinking that if he did he would become an invalid.

Winter golf at Lincoln Hills. Left to right: Len Edmondson, Karl Schwaibold, John Carney and his dog "Speedy". (Courtesy Ludington Daily News)

Lee Edmondson was Len's son and was only about 16 when Len died. Lee took up where his father left off and won the club championship five straight years starting when he was in high school in 1966. Lee attended Michigan State University and was All-America in golf while in college. He then became a golf pro in the St. Louis area during the summer while working as a ski pro in Aspen in the winter.

There have been other multiple winners through the years including Russ Wilson, Paul Kolinski, Jerry Ponko Jr., Charley Peterson, Dick Gretzinger, Brian Boals, and Dan Motyka, who won the championship a remarkable nine times. Greg Magee won it four straight years as the most gifted long-term pupil of our professional Tom Baldwin.

The ladies have had a club champion since 1942. The most accomplished of these was Barbara Rohn Harrington, who won the championship 27 times. Barb also played in district and state competitions. Carole Schierholt has also won the championship 16 times including a run of five straight in recent years.

A Member-Guest Tournament associated with a Calcutta has been popular at Lincoln Hills for many years. In 1990 the Codger Tournament was inaugurated for the seniors. It involved different partnership formats, including better ball and alternate shot play. It has been a popular annual event with the older members, and its openings are always filled. One problem with both of these events has been slow play. Many of the participants seem to think that they are playing in a national event and they line up their putts from every angle. Six hour rounds are not unusual.

The Stagoree was a yearly event for a while. It could have been spelled Staggeree. Players were solicited from other clubs, and there was generally a large crowd attending. Circles were drawn around the cup with lime on some of the par 3s, and players were urged to bet and to try their luck in hitting their tee shots inside the circle. Little six ounce beers were available free at several strategic locations around the course. The custom was to drink one and to take one with you at each station. The last Stagoree that I played in took us 7 hours to finish 18 holes. With an even beer level all afternoon I had 6 pars, 6 birdies, and 6 bogies in that round. A cookout always followed the golf, and there were great door-prizes. The event annually raised about a thousand dollars for the club. It was finally dropped from the club schedule, but a female version called the Lollapalooza survives.

My favorite tournament was the Father and Son, which in later years was expanded to include many other categories of partnerships such as Father and Daughter and Grandparent and Grandchild. The tournament was played in a kind of two-ball foursome format which I have heard called "greensomes". Both parties drove on each hole. The better drive was selected, and from then on the players played alternate shots. When the chemistry was right, the cooperative effort was a beautiful thing, but golf being the game that it is, this situation seldom happened. When things went wrong in the partnership, both hostility and guilt tended to surface, and that made things even worse.

My son John and I won this tournament seven times. On one occasion we were seven under par for a stretch of eleven holes.

We shot 67 that day. It was the lowest score ever made in that tournament and was one of my five greatest thrills in nearly eighty years of golf. The others were my first hole-in-one on what is now the fifteenth, winning my first senior club championship, shooting 69 in a medal tournament, and making a 71 at the age of 83. All these events occurred at Lincoln Hills.

The best player ever to play Lincoln Hills regularly was Jay Baumgartner, a summer visitor from Bristol, Tennessee. Jay held the course record of 61 when the par was 70. He was a player without a weakness. He was a force in southern amateur golfing circles Once I noted in the newspapers that Jay was a semi-finalist in the North and South Amateur in Pinehurst, one of the most prestigious of the country's amateur championships. I think that Lee Edmondson was the second best player in Lincoln Hills' history.

The first course record holder at Lincoln Hills was Louis Montedonico, an Epworth member, who shot a 66 in 1924 when par was 67. This record score was equaled by a professional Laurie Ayton, in an exhibition match against the famous Jock Hutchinson in 1926. Ayton shot the same score again when the pair returned in 1928. The Lincoln Hills pro, Larry Weichman, tied that record in 1930 and later in the year shot 65, 64 and eventually 63.

Fred Couples played Lincoln Hills once in the 1980s while staying at Epworth where his wife's family had a cottage. Fred played the course, but did not putt, feeling that the comparative slowness and roughness of the greens even at that late date would be harmful to his putting stroke. Paul Hahn came to Lincoln Hills once to give an exhibition of trick shots and a tour player, Dave Ragan, also gave an exhibition.

There is a note in the Lincoln Hills log in 1938 about a high school golf team playing at the club. This team sport was abandoned, but around 1962 Hal Madden, who was at times coach, athletic director, and assistant superintendent at Ludington area schools revived the activity and coached a Ludington High School golf team again. Hal remembers that some of his first players were Gerald Ponko Jr., Tom Bourrisseau and Roger Boals. Hal disbanded the team when the boys failed to practice and to attend team meetings. A year or so later a new group of boys including Lee

Edmondson, Jon Hartman, Hal's son Kurt, "Budde" Reed and John Carney Jr. went to Hal asking him to revive the team. This team was among the best in the state for the next several years.

Ludington High School re-established golf as a varsity sport in 1962 and it has continued uninterrupted ever since. Pictured here from left to right are Lee Edmondson, John Carney Jr., Kurt Madden, John Quinn and Budde Reed.

Recently another group of talented young golfers has surfaced, including Aaron Klemm and Luke Sniegowski. They have made themselves known in state high school golfing circles. Besides Madden, Walt Zbojniewicz, Don Peterson, and others have served as coaches of Ludington High School golf teams. More recently Ludington has had a girl's golf team. Our present pro, Tom Baldwin, has held clinics for young golfers, teaching them the basics and the etiquette of the game. These efforts will help to develop younger golfers to replace those of my generation who are disappearing from the scene.

Several of our younger golfers have been talented enough to become professionals. Besides Lee Edmondson, Tom Leafstrand was a golf pro in Kansas, Jimmy Holmes is a long-time professional at a club in Chicago, and Ted Tallefson was an assistant at Oakland Hills and is now the head pro at Muskegon Country Club.

Joe Kowatch is a teaching pro at a club near Turin, Italy. Most recently Erica Bieniek is our first female member to turn professional after an outstanding college golfing career at Western Michigan University.

CHAPTER XV
CADDIES

Caddies have always been a part of golf. Before the advent of the pull-cart and gas and electric riding carts, caddies were a necessity unless a golfer wanted to carry his own clubs. The caddy was not only a beast of burden, he searched for balls, was an observer and a sort of companion, and at the most professional level he gave advice and information about distances, club selection and method of play. Caddies have largely disappeared from the American golfing scene except on the professional tours and at expensive private clubs and resorts. There, as well as in Europe, caddies are often grown men who make their living at the trade.

Since I preferred to walk and carry my bag, my experience with caddies was limited, but I did meet a few of these older characters along the way. We had a gray-haired black caddy with cataracts at Southern Pines in North Carolina. He was wearing a long coat on that warm day. As we left the first tee I asked him if he had seen our drives. He said, "No Suh! But Ah knows where they is!" And he did!

One story, whose truth I cannot vouch for involved an elderly black caddy working for an unpleasant golfer. The golfer complained bitterly about gnats flying around his head. The caddy remarked, "Dem is fuzz flies. Dey hang around horses' asses." The golfer sputtered, "Are you calling me a horse's ass?" "Oh no, Suh! But you can't fool dem fuzz flies!"

At the Old Course at St. Andrews in Scotland we employed a grizzled veteran named Hutchinson who had a white dog with him on a leash. He regaled us with his life story while we were waiting to tee off. With his brogue and a delivery like bursts of machine gun fire, he was difficult to understand, but we gleaned the following: He had two dogs which had made his fortune by finding golf balls. He had trained them by heating balls and having them smell them. As far as we could understand him, his white dog found balls on the ground and his black dog found them in the air!

When we were out of sight of the starter's shack, he released the dog from its leash, and it loped down the fairways after every errant drive, dove into the prickly gorse, and each time came out with the ball in its mouth. The caddy would say, "Gi' me a ba'" and the dog would bring one back either from the whins or from the fairway of the New Course adjacent. When we told the caddy that these latter balls were not lost, but were in play on the other course, he developed a deaf ear and proceeded heedlessly onward.

I had a native caddy without shoes in Barbados in the 50s. His sensitive feet located balls in the deep rough. He told me how to approach each green and indicated the line I should take on putts, using his big toe as the indicator. I played well but derived no satisfaction from it, feeling that I was only the tool of the caddy's expertise.

During the early years of Lincoln Hills Golf Club, the caddies were exclusively boys and young men who used their earnings for the little luxuries that made life more pleasant. During the Depression years there was little money for sweets, movies, and other non-necessities. The boys who caddied not only earned a little spending money, they earned it in the fresh air and sunshine in attractive surroundings and generally in the company of nice people. Importantly they were introduced to the customs, etiquette, and rules of golf. Most of them practiced and played golf in between caddying jobs and many of them continued to play for the rest of their lives.

A number of our older members were introduced to golf in this way. We know nothing of the caddies of the 20s and early 30s, since they are all gone and have left no record. We know that in the mid-thirties there were groups of caddies at both Epworth and Lincoln Hills. They tended to work at one place or the other and did not usually shift back and forth except when an Epworth member took his favorite caddy to Lincoln Hills with him. There were caddy-masters at both courses to see to it that the little rascals behaved themselves and to oversee their assignments and professional adequacy.

Russ Wilson was the caddy-master at Lincoln Hills in the thirties, and Jimmy Montedonico had the same job and collected green fees at Epworth. The Montedonicos were wealthy Epworth residents and Jimmy may not have been paid for his efforts. He was good to his boys and let them play golf and tennis when there was no business and the course and the courts were vacant.

The caddies avoided some players, especially the slow, the unskilled, the quirky, and the unpleasant ones. Of course they avoided the poor tippers. When one of these showed up, the caddies disappeared until the undesirable person had gone. Bob Erickson was one of the caddies at Epworth. He was the youngest caddy there, didn't know enough to hide when the women came around, and got stuck with one young woman for some four-hour nine hole rounds. Jimmy Montedonico nicknamed him "Fish" for getting caught by these ladies and the name stuck for the rest of his life.

While some of the caddies did not like caddying for women unless they were young and beautiful, one of my friends regularly caddied for them and made a good thing of it. He never failed to compliment them on their game. "Your swing is so much better today, Mrs. Jones!" "Why thank you, Ronnie!" And after one of those interminable par five holes when the lady asked, "Did I make a ten or an eleven, Ronnie?", he always answered, "I only counted seven." "Oh, good!" Ronnie always got a big tip.

Some of the Lincoln Hills caddies in the 30s were John and Dick Meissner, Dale Speidel, Roger and Everett Liebetreu, LeRoy Johnson, Mickey Phillips, and Howard Genson. Dick Meissner remembers that they were paid 70 cents a round to caddy. If they were lucky, they earned a dollar with the tip, but never more than that. Dick remembers caddying double for 36 holes one Fourth of July. He thought that he was the richest guy in the world when he walked away with four whole dollars.

The caddies played poker using tees to gamble with because they had no money. New caddies were hazed and were regularly thrown into the Lincoln River by their more experienced peers until they were accepted. When they weren't busy, they often swam off the Dummy Bridge. The Lincoln Hills caddies disparagingly referred to the short Epworth course as "The Pea Patch."

The carrying of clubs was a different problem in those days. The rule which limits players to 14 clubs was not passed by the USGA until 1938 and by the R&A until 1939. Some players carried as many as 20 or 25 clubs. Some had left-handed clubs for unusual situations, and multiple putters, cleeks, and chippers. Placed in a large leather bag, this made a heavy burden for the caddies. Fortunately not all golfers were like that. Many of us had "Sunday bags", which were small light canvas affairs which held only a few clubs.

When Chick Evans won the United States Open in 1916 and set a scoring record which lasted for generations, he carried only nine clubs. About 1935, I played golf several times with Carlton Wells, a University of Michigan English professor who was a friend of Chick Evans. Professor Wells had been Michigan Amateur Champion ten years before and had given up the game. He started playing again with me, and it was eye-opening. Wells had a Sunday bag and five hickory-shafted clubs, a brassie, a mid-iron, a mashie, a niblick, and a putter. He played some difficult courses scoring around 80, often making half shots with each of his clubs to make up for the gaps between them.

Arthur Anderson of the famous accounting firm was a kindly man and was called "Pop" by the caddies, but he apparently was one of those people who could not communicate with others without touching them. The caddies didn't like that and they all avoided him, except for Vernon Fitch and another boy whom the old caddies think was Roger Liebetreu. These two caddied for him regularly. As a result Anderson paid for Fitch's education at the University of Michigan, and he also paid for the college expenses of the other boy.

One of the old-time caddies at Epworth was Clayton "Izzy" Schwartz. Clayton became a competent golfer, but he was so frustrated by his inability to achieve perfection and by his resulting violent outbursts of temper that he quit golf for 25 years. When he resumed playing again, he reacted to his bad shots with gales of laughter. He had learned to treat the same problem with a different emotion.

In 1949 an abandoned railroad shelter was brought from the defunct Dummy Line onto Lincoln Hills and set up north and west of the clubhouse, and it served for many years as a caddy shack. In 1951 Charles Paukstis Jr. was hired as caddy-master for $16 per week. In addition, he was authorized to collect 5 cents for each nine holes from each caddy and 5 cents from the club for each nine holes in which a golf pull-cart was rented. Charles says that the caddies rarely paid him. John Pomeroy and his brother Paul caddied at Lincoln Hills during that era along with Don Sanders and Jim McCumber. John regularly caddied for Bub Starke. By then caddy fees had reached a dollar, and they often got a two bit tip.

One caddy job which has disappeared was the shagging of practice balls. Dick Meissner remembers that one Epworth client bought a dozen Wilson Walker Cups, the cheapest ball available. He would knock them out and Dick would shag them and bring them back to him.

In the 60s another group of boys caddied regularly at Lincoln Hills. All of them were golfers, and included Kurt Madden, Budde Reed, Jimmy Holmes, and John Carney Jr.

Every course has stories about its caddies. Once, an Epworth guest employed one of the local boys to caddy for him at Lincoln Hills. The player purchased a dozen Titleists before the round and handed eleven of them to the caddy to deposit in his bag. This was too great a temptation for the caddy, who was himself an enthusiastic golfer and has since turned professional. As the round progressed, the caddy began squirreling the new balls away in strategic places around the course where he could go back later and pick them up. By the time the group reached the 18th hole, all eleven unplayed balls had been so deposited. It was hard to lose a ball on the 18th, but the guest managed to do so, perhaps running his ball down a gopher hole. He put out his hand, snapping his fingers and saying, "Give me another ball, boy". The caddy was embarrassed and said, "We don't have any, sir!" The guest exploded, and ultimately the caddy complained to his friends that the cheap so-and-so didn't even tip him a dime.

CHAPTER XVI
DISASTERS ON THE GOLF COURSE

There is more than one version of the greatest disaster which occurred at a local golf course. What exactly happened is not entirely clear. Arthur Anderson played golf regularly at Epworth. His summer home and his daughter's lay near one of the greens. Anderson's granddaughter, blond blue-eyed, seven year old Suzie Johnson was accustomed to run up to the green at Epworth to greet her grandfather as his group approached it. One version is that on July 4, 1945 she did this and was struck in the temple by a golf ball which was hit toward the green.

Our initial information was that she was killed instantly. But further delving revealed that she was taken to Hackley Hospital in Muskegon and later to a Chicago hospital where she died on July 12th following a convulsion. This type of injury generally causes a skull fracture and a tear in the middle meningeal artery with a resulting extradural hematoma. The classic symptoms are of immediate loss of consciousness, followed by a brief lucid period and then a deep coma. Treatment is by immediately putting burr holes in the skull to evacuate the blood in order to relieve the pressure on the brain. This is a major life-threatening emergency.

In the 1950s I attended a two week post-graduate surgical course at Cook County Hospital along with my friend and classmate Dr. Tom Barton from Howell, Michigan. A Chicago neurosurgeon lectured to us about injuries of the type suffered by Suzie Johnson. He said, "This is an extreme emergency. There is no time to transport the patient to the specialist 60 miles away. You must immediately put a burr hole in the skull, and if you don't find blood there, you must put another burr hole on the opposite side!" He then told us exactly what kind of a drill and burrs to purchase. I came out of the lecture gung-ho to buy this equipment, but Tom said to me, "John, are you crazy? If you go around putting burr holes in people's skulls in Ludington, they're going to ride you out of town on a rail! If you see an injury of that type, the person's just going to die!" Fortunately in 42 years of practice, I never once saw such a case.

It was never determined whose shot had struck Suzie. The golf course layout was changed to eliminate a blind tee shot as a result of this accident, and Anderson was so affected by the tragedy that he put his cottage up for sale the next day, quit golf, and left Epworth and never returned. He died in 1947.

We had one fatality at Lincoln Hills, and it is the only one that we have heard of occurring there. One of the golfers complained of chest pain to his partners during the round, and his group, which included an attorney, played on without him and left him sitting by himself on a bench on the 6th tee. When the next group arrived on the tee, they found that the player had collapsed and was lying on the ground pulseless. Dr. Charles Paukstis was in that second group and he performed CPR, but to no avail. When the golfer arrived in the ER, he was dead and I could not resuscitate him.

I thought that abandoning this man while he was suffering a heart attack displayed an almost unbelievably callous attitude by this man's companions. Their behavior was even worse than that of George's friends in the old story about the golfer who returned from the course in a state of utter exhaustion. The player's wife asked him what had happened. He replied, "We had a perfectly awful day. George had a heart attack on the second tee. After that it was hit the ball and drag George, hit the ball and drag George all day long!"

John Pomeroy fared much better when he had a cardiac arrest on the course in recent years. John had previously had a major heart attack. Dr. Kang Hoon Lee was playing in his foursome when John's heart arrested, and he performed CPR and called for an ambulance on his cell phone, and John survived unscathed. He now has an implanted defibrillator which has gone off on several occasions, leaving him badly shaken but still alive.

Recently, Chris Bentz spotted Byron Higgins lying on his face on the 3rd tee while Bud Johnson was ministering to him. By the time we had run over to help, Byron was sitting up and had a strong regular pulse at a normal rate. He told us that he had birdied the previous hole and then suddenly had found himself lying face down on the ground. Byron had scraped his face severely in the fall, and that was suspicious of a serious problem, because simple fainting usually gives enough warning so that a person can cushion his fall, whereas when a person's heart stops, there is no warning and that person drops like a rock. Byron later had another similar spell. These are called Stokes-Adams attacks and result when the heart's conduction system fails completely. When this happens, there is often a period of asystole [no heart-beat] before the ventricles start beating on their own. Byron is now sporting a pacemaker and should be good for another decade or so.

Medicine has made huge strides in the cardiac field in the last half century with pacemakers, defibrillators, coronary care units, coronary by-passes, angioplasties, stress tests, echocardiograms, and other diagnostic and therapeutic tools which allow many of us with cardiac problems who would have died of them during the first half of the Twentieth Century to now lead long and full lives.

CHAPTER XVII
WAGERING

Betting is an essential part of golf. You can be sure that if there is a golf course in Heaven, St. Peter will be playing for money, golf balls or for cups of nectar. For most of us the amounts involved are inconsequential. Even the smallest wager is worth playing for, and it is the concept of winning or losing rather than the amount that is important. The multi-millionaire who wins two dollars on the golf course must be paid. It is a debt of honor.

Although there are some high rollers, most of us at Lincoln Hills play for modest stakes. It is a curious thing, but the people I play with still play for the same amounts that we did when I arrived here nearly sixty years ago, although the actual value of the stakes is only about $1/20^{th}$ of what it was at the earlier time. If there are no bets and a golfer makes a triple-bogie on the first hole, thus making a good score unlikely, there is little incentive for him to continue the round.

We have played a variety of games throughout the years. The most popular were partnership games, either a single better ball score for the partnership or high-low for two points on each hole. Before there were reliable handicaps, we sometimes chose partners by pairing the high and the low players at the end of four holes. To make this work well, we had to depend on the integrity of each golfer to play his best and not jockey for position. This was put to the test the first time that I played with Jay Baumgartner. Kim Berger was usually a skillful player, but he had an awful start that day. As I became aware of how good Jay was, it dawned on me why Kim was playing so poorly.

We had a rule that the winners bought the drinks. Once I faced a short birdie putt on the last green. If I made it, my partner and I would win ten cents, and this would not go far toward paying for the drinks. My putt sort of dribbled down and died near the hole. One of my opponents, Walter "ZeeZee" Zbojniewicz, a Dow chemist, turned on his heel disgustedly and said, "I've seen better acts than that in a whorehouse!"

Kim and I won quite a large sum from Reg Chadwick, who sold tombstones, and Jerry Walter one day. I was called away medically right after the round and couldn't stay for the libations. Kim was to split the winnings with me. But when they got done drinking, there was nothing left to split. Reg and Jerry had met the challenge.

Some golfers go to extremes for strokes, L to R, Jack Schillinger, Herman Yoder, John Carney, Harry Eastman, Jerry Ponko, Jr., Don Baldwin, Kim Burger and Karl Schwaibold.

We played a number of different games. The worst of them was Bingo-Bango-Bongo. This game was supposed to equalize the odds for players of different skills, but it lead to the most egregious jockeying for points. Bingo was first on the green. Bango was closest to the pin when all the balls were on the green. Bongo was first in the cup.

We played proxies, also called greenies [closest to the pin in regulation], sneakers [one putt pars], and sandy sneakers or sandies [the same out of a bunker]. There were sometimes disagreements over interpretations of the rules on these bets. I made an eagle three on what is now the second hole one day, but Harry Eastman would not give me a proxy, which he interpreted as closest to the hole in regulation and on the green. He said that my third shot was not on the green. It was in the cup *in* the green! On another occasion there was a blow-up which I witnessed as Harry's foursome played through us. Judge Charley Carroll had made a par out of a bunker, but Harry would not give him a sandy sneaker, because after his shot from the bunker his ball was not actually lying on the putting surface!

Some of the guys were hard bargainers, and matches were often won or lost on the first tee. Harry Eastman and Ben Peterson, a retired Cadillac dealer, were notorious for this. Once I witnessed them tee off together in the same group, and I said to myself, "This will never work". Sure enough, within five minutes Harry was back at the clubhouse. He and Ben couldn't come to any agreement on the bets.

The first tee was generally the site for a litany of complaints. "My back hurts." "I've got tennis elbow." "I've been up all night." These complaints were generally met with indifference by the opposition. But my great friend Dr. Chuck Kagay, who often visited us from Hilton Head, had been near death with a rare sarcoma and wore a colostomy bag as well as a ureterostomy bag. We used these effectively to get not only sympathy for him but also some sucker bets.

Chuck could bring tears to your eyes with accounts of his nine-hour surgery and his eight subsequent operations. He said after his first ordeal, "I didn't hear the fat lady sing, but I heard her clearing her throat!" Later he said, "I get up in the morning and look at this awful face in the mirror. Then I breathe on the mirror and if it clouds up I know I'm not dead!" When he developed the exceedingly painful tic doloureux, he said, "I've heard of people with this jumping out of the window and I considered it, but then I realized that the window was only three feet above the ground".

Fair competition depended on the honesty of the competitors. If the handicaps were properly figured and all the scores were factored in, there were usually quite even results, and over the long run little money changed hands even between the big bettors. A few golfers do not report their good scores, saying that they are uncharacteristic. Others do the same with their bad scores, trying to boast of a lower handicap than they are entitled to. We call the first group "sand-baggers". The world could do without them. Those in the second group are the suckers.

When I was young, Joe Louis was the Heavyweight Champion of the World. He was naïve and he had earned millions of dollars with his boxing. He was the sucker whom all the Detroit area black entrepreneurs took for a ride. He and his entourage regularly came to the University Golf Course in Ann Arbor on Sundays, and his hangers-on, who probably had touring professional golfing skills, plucked him regularly while giving him hope by occasionally letting him win and by keeping the matches close. His advisors, the IRS and all of these "friends" put him into a negative financial position from which there was no escape.

I always thought that high-roller gambling was incompatible with the essence of golf. Golf was itself absorbing enough and challenging enough that it didn't need big-time gambling to keep one's interest. To me the emphasis in the big-time game was not on the competition and on winning and losing, but on money and on separating the opposition from it. These people would have derived the same thrill from poker or a crap game.

Big money games tended to encourage golfers to subject their opponent's play to scrutiny and to charges of minor rules infractions with resulting penalties. I hate clubhouse lawyers, and to me, unless you are playing in a tournament, fooling around with ticky-tacky rules infractions and penalties spoils the game and causes hard feelings. Rigid rules are probably necessary in tournament golf, but the Rules of Golf and their interpretations and decisions are so complicated that even touring professionals don't know or understand them. I never called a penalty against an opponent in my life. To me fairness and intent should be the important features of rulings as well as whether the violation gives a significant advantage to the perpetrator. Count your strokes, and play the ball as it lies are the important rules to me.

If I won a match, I wanted to have won because I had played better than my opponent or because I was luckier than he was. I did not want to win because of penalty strokes resulting from my having discovered that my opponent was carrying an extra club, that he had asked me or looked to see what club I had used, or that his ball had moved a fraction of an inch after he had addressed it.

It amazes me that The Ten Commandments which tell us how to live our entire lives comprise only a portion of one page in the Bible, while the rules of a small segment of life called golf take up so much space. So, tongue-in-cheek, I have composed The Ten Commandments of Golf in the Appendix, listing in simple terms how most of us play golf these days.

I only heard of one Ludington man who may have been done in financially by golf. He was a pharmacist who came to Ludington from Chicago to take over the City Drug Store. When he arrived, he trumpeted his 3 handicap, which established him among the elite golfers of the club. He had a beautiful swing and drove the ball well, but the rest of his game was far below this standard. Ben Peterson and others like him plucked this gentleman regularly, and it was not long before he departed, having been wagered out of his drug-store, according to rumor.

I recall the most lop-sided match that I ever played in. My son and I were playing against Lee Edmondson and Shirley Myers. Lee was only about 12 or 13 and was a Tiger-like golfing prodigy. We played all the garbage like proxies and double on birdies. Lee had been constantly complaining because his partner had been hitting it so close that he was taking the proxies away from Lee. Things were going badly for us and the atmosphere was grim. Finally on the 14th tee Lee piped up with, "Mr. Myers, are we 26 up or 27 up?" I responded with. "Ya little shit, I'm never going to play golf with you again!"

But I relented, and we played a lot of golf together through the years. I was Lee's best man at his wedding in St. Louis. I was playing with Lee the day he first broke 70. He was about 14 at the time. In those days we didn't say, "Good Job!" every time our kids wet their pants. Lee ran over to his father as Len was coming off the 9th green. He exclaimed, "Dad, I just shot 68!" Len never broke stride or said a word. He just grunted and went on.

CHAPTER XVIII
MEMORIES AND MUSINGS ON THE PAST

As I look back over sixty years of membership in Lincoln Hills Golf Club, I recall not only a very different golf course, clubhouse and clientele, but also different customs and activities. By 1950, there was an active social life among the members with dances and dinner-dances on Saturday nights. The membership was younger in those days, and driving a car under the influence was not as seriously regarded as it is today. There was heavier drinking at these events than nowadays. Sunday morning was devoted to men's golf, and there were many red eyes on the first tee.

The club had no starting times in those days, and the first tee was generally crowded in the morning hours on week-ends. A slanted tube was located on the first tee, and the first member of each foursome to arrive on the tee ran a ball down the tube. When the ball reached the bottom of the tube and was removed by its owner, his foursome was on the tee.

The opening tee shot on Sunday mornings by the hung-over golfers was often spectacularly bad, causing great hilarity among the spectators. In those days, we wore our pants with cuffs. One member, who was a reasonably able golfer, hit his opening tee shot into his pants cuff.

There was a lot of chit-chat on the first tee. On one occasion, the greens-keeper Rick Grunch's skinny mangy hound was on the tee with his leg above his head licking himself. One of the more clever spectators commented, "I wish I could do that." George Michael "Peck" Pomeroy said, "Why not, Jack? I don't think the dog would mind."

Wednesday was men's day and there was usually a stag dinner on Wednesday evenings. Sometimes a program was presented afterwards. There was always a poker game in the evening. Some of us played golf matches after dinner using only one club.

There were home and home matches with Manistee, and these sometimes occasioned some serious drinking. I played once with a Manistee member who started the round playing quite respectably, but by the end was so drunk that he was hardly able to hit his ball out of his shadow. One member became so inebriated at a Manistee outing that his friends stuffed him into a locker and left him there while they went in to eat dinner.

After a stag, one of the older lawyers left the clubhouse reeling into the parking lot ready to drive himself home. I ran into the clubhouse seeking the help of another attorney in getting this man home safely. His reply was that I was not to worry and that his colleague could drive when he couldn't walk. He did in fact get home without incident.

Some golf clubs make an attempt to encourage mixing of the foursomes especially on men's day. At one club I know of, the men arrive at the club without a game on Wednesdays and the pro makes up the foursomes as the golfers appear. At another, golfers sign up individually on a time sheet. These customs promote camaraderie among the club members. Lincoln Hills, and to an extent Ludington in general, has tended to be cliquish. Members usually divide into groups of four and sometimes a multiple of that number and continue to play with that same group year after year. At Lincoln Hills, the chief mixer has been the club tournaments. The handicap tournament particularly paired golfers of all levels of skill together in fair competition.

One group, which played together for years, was called "The Gruesome Foursome" and consisted of Don Hack, Jerry Walter, Reg Chadwick, and Ed Casperson. This group mixed alcohol with golf, and the players had unusual and spectacular ways of distracting each other during the round. Talking or moving during an opponent's backswing was a common practice. They dropped golf balls on the green during an opponent's putting stroke. It was not unusual to hear a firecracker explode while someone in their foursome was playing a shot. Don Hack was a good player, but his handicap was much higher than it should have been because of the adverse circumstances under which he usually played. He was a tough opponent in handicap tournaments, since he usually scored considerably lower when he played with people with normal golfing etiquette.

Reg Chadwick did some of that to me one day, dropping a golf ball "kerplunk" on to the green during my putting stroke. When he putted next, he found me walking back and forth beyond the hole directly in his line. He stopped and said, "What are you doing?" I told him, "If you pull that stuff on me again, you're going to find me walking around here all day long." He didn't do it any more. Reg talked funny. He spoke rapidly and jerkily in a sort of half stammer. When I played golf with him and with John Pomeroy one day, John said to me as we left the ninth tee, "I'm never going to play golf with this SOB again. I can't understand a thing he says, so I just agree with him. Some time that's going to be the wrong thing to do, and he's going to pop me in the nose!"

I was intrigued by a foursome of former club champions that was a regular on weekends at Lincoln Hills for years. The foursome consisted of Bub Starke, an industrialist, Russ Wilson, a butcher, Len Edmondson, a retailer, and Louis Anderson, a bookkeeper. As far as I could see, they had nothing in common except that they were the four best golfers in town. I thought that it was neat that their love of golf was so strong that it overrode any differences in social status, personality, or outside interests.

Ben Bourisseau was the long-time probate judge and an occasional golfer at Lincoln Hills. Ben was very deaf, and he used his hearing aid to his advantage on the golf course. He loved to needle his golfing companions, and when they tried to retaliate verbally he turned off his hearing aid and they couldn't get through to him at all. Two of his companions got even with him at one of the stags. They sat across from him at the table, and one of them started telling the other a fictional tale about a trip he had made to Chicago. As he described taking a young woman up to his room and the details that followed, he began gradually dropping his voice. Ben was leaning across the table all ears. Eventually only the man's lips were moving and no sound was coming out at all. Ben was banging on his hearing aid, shaking it and checking the connections. Paybacks are hell.

Claude "Bud" Shanks Jr. was one of our more unusual members. Bud was a huge man weighing, I would guess, around 400 pounds. His uncle Andy, a massive man, had been a professional boxer in the early part of the Twentieth Century. I believe that Andy Shanks was the Michigan State Heavyweight Boxing Champion. Bud had been a collegiate football lineman at Bowling Green University. He loved to tease Hal Madden, who had been an opponent on the line at Central Michigan. He told Hal, "Our bread and butter play was 'Number 38 through Madden'." Once when we were on a golf trip, Bud tripped and fell down on a green. I wasn't sure that the other three of us would ever be able to get him back on his feet again.

We were playing golf near Kalamazoo one day and were behind a foursome of rough-looking characters. Bud was waiting on the tee for these men who were strung out all over the course. Someone suggested to Bud that he go ahead and drive. Bud declined saying, "Those guys look like they might give me a cement shoe." One of us said, "Maybe you could outrun them!" The incredulous look on Bud's face was just like the one that Jackie Gleason used when Art Carney said something outrageous.

I played Bud in the finals of my last Senior Club Championship. Neither of us had any reason to be there, because Clayton Schaner was easily the best player in the tournament. But Bud had shot an uncharacteristic round in the 70s in his semi-final match against Clayton. Clayton had a tendency to get bent out of shape when things didn't go according to plan, and he didn't respond with his usual game. When we played, Bud had one of those awful days that occur occasionally on the golf course. He said later that he had felt intimidated, I suppose by the Super Sunday atmosphere. He picked up on each of the first four holes, conceding each hole. My reputation with the short stick was not a good one, and walking up the fifth fairway one of our fellow players commented to Bud, "Well, I'd at least make him putt!"

Once I played a match against Nate Graham's son. When his wife and child arrived on the first tee to watch, I knew I had an advantage. And when Nate and his wife Alpha arrived a few holes later to put additional pressure on him, I knew I was going to win. Obviously Nate had told his son about my putting reputation because he conceded nothing while I gave him two-footers all day long. Finally on the 14th green he gave me a deciding downhill side hill putt for the match. I wouldn't have conceded that putt to my best friend! A miss would have rolled off the green.

Although I was a terrible yippy putter on the course, I was not that bad on the practice green. One day I had a two hour putting match with Lee Edmondson. I crowed as he was paying me off, "Everyone in the club is going to hear about this!" He said, "Listen! Only two of us know about it and nobody will believe you!"

Once I drove the 18th green 300 yards away and made the putt for an eagle two. When I told Ralph Cerny, the CEO of the hospital, about it, he said, "I believe you drove the green, but I don't believe you made the putt."

I played golf with one of the less accomplished club members one day. He was terrible and he shaved a stroke or two off his score on nearly every hole. He was so bad that it didn't make any difference, so I never said anything. It was at least a couple of years before I played with him again. His game had substantially improved in the meantime. He commented to me, "I feel like I'm playing so much better, but I'm not scoring any better!" I didn't say anything, but I thought that it was a lot harder to cheat when you are making 4, 5, and 6 than when you are making 7, 8, and 9.

Leroy Hinspeter was a Dow engineer and was the golfer described in the Preface shooting 71 while hitting only one green in regulation. On another occasion, things were not going nearly as well for him. He suffered every bad bounce, found every bunker, was up against tree trunks, and lipped out his putts. As we left the 7th green, ZeeZee commented to him, "Leroy, with your luck if you fell into a barrel of teats, you'd come out sucking your thumb!"

There was no dress code in those days, beyond any illegal or immoral exposure of the body. Most of us had been taught by our parents that sunshine was beneficial to our health, supplying us with vitamin D. So during the summer months many of us stripped to the waist in order to get a sun tan while we played. There was no ban on fabrics or styles of clothing.

Lincoln Hills was largely a male bastion at that time. Women played, but not to the extent that they do now. Thursday was Ladies Day. Women did not play on Wednesdays, and women and children were discouraged from playing on weekend mornings. In those days, women were considered to be slow players who

THE HISTORY OF LINCOLN HILLS GOLF CLUB: One Man's Perspective

might hold up the rest of the course, and most of them could play on any other day. The men had to work all week, so that they had first choice on the weekends.

For many years we had a starter and ranger named Herb Nordquist who was a retired policeman from Detroit. Herb was diplomatic and was a favorite around the club. By that time the women of the club had learned to play faster. They not only kept up, but they themselves were now irritated by slow play. One day a group of women was distressed by the deliberation of the men ahead of them. They persuaded Herb, who was off duty, to speak to these men and hurry them up. After talking to the men, Herb returned and told the women, "They said that if they played as well as you are playing, they'd play faster!" The women stopped complaining and were all smiles after that.

Sometimes the women played home and home matches with other clubs. There was a disagreement among two of the women during a match with Cadillac Country Club. A Cadillac woman announced that she had taken an 11 on a certain hole. Her Ludington opponent disagreed saying that she had counted 12. They went over each stroke. The Ludington player said, "You whiffed that one." Her opponent said, "No, that was a practice swing." The Ludington lady asked, "Do you generally say, 'Oh shit!' when you take a practice swing?"

Bobby Jones was not only a great golfer, but he was recognized as one of the finest gentlemen in the history of the game. Yet he wrote that until the end of his golfing days there were some shots which he could not finish holding the club in his hands. One day I was walking by the woods behind what is now the third green. A foursome was combing the woods. I stopped and asked them what was wrong. They replied that Jerry Ponko, Jr. had four-putted the green below. He had hurled his putter into the trees and they couldn't find it. I walked into the woods, picked up the putter and handed it to Jerry. His comment was, "See what experience will do for you!"

Young Jerry was the object of ridicule in the funniest episode that I witnessed at Lincoln Hills. He was not only the club champion but the longest hitter in the club. His drives from the southpaw side were legendary, starting low and still rising as they soared past the

250 yard mark. It was opening day at the club. Several of the high-school teachers, who were new members, were standing on the tee as Jerry prepared to hit his first shot of the year. I told the teachers to watch closely and they would witness one of the longest tee shots they had ever seen. When Jerry took his first swing he hit the ground at least a foot behind the ball, which trickled just a few inches off the peg. The shot, after that build-up, was too much for the teachers, who all fell to the ground and rolled around convulsed with laughter. The last time I reminded Jerry of that shot, he threw his driver at me.

Another interesting incident occurred when I played golf with Jeff Dorrell. Jeff had been a promising athlete and an exceptional tennis player when as a teen-ager he developed an osteogenic sarcoma in his right arm. The surgeons amputated his arm, disarticulating it at the shoulder. Subsequent to the surgery, Jeff developed several metastases to his lungs. Each of these was treated at the Mayo Clinic by resecting a portion of his lung. Jeff thought that he was going to die and lived his life on the edge like the hero in the old TV show "Run for Your Life". Among other things, he did trick skiing in Colorado doing somersaults and revolutions in the air.

On the day of the incident, we drove off what is now the 13th tee. The hill had not yet been removed, and it was a blind tee shot. When we got over the hill, we found the high school golf team in the fairway waiting to hit their second shots. Jeff had hit his drive over their heads. Jeff was most apologetic, saying, "Gee, I'm sorry fellows. We didn't know you were down here." What interested me was the look of chagrin on the young golfers' faces when they saw that the man who had out-driven them by so much had an empty right sleeve.

Jeff eventually realized that he was going to live and that he'd better find a way to earn his living. He went to college to become an agronomist and became the greens-keeper of The Rose, a golf course near Cadillac. Unfortunately he recently succumbed to a second unrelated cancer.

I have many pleasant memories of the golfers with whom I have played at Lincoln Hills. Among these friends and companions were Hal Madden, who played golf with me for 56 years; Herman

THE HISTORY OF LINCOLN HILLS GOLF CLUB: One Man's Perspective

Yoder, who accompanied me on many golfing trips to Scotland, Ireland, and England as well as to the Southern United States; Kim Berger; Peck Pomeroy; Gerald Ponko Sr.; Karl Schwaibold; Father William McKnight; Don Baldwin, the school superintendent; Walt Zbojniewicz; Ben Peterson; Jack Maskal; Garth Belland; Bill McPike; Chris Bentz; Dick Rathsack; and many others.

More than half of these men are dead, and all the rest, except the last two, have quit golf, at least at Lincoln Hills. For twenty years or so, twelve of us played together three times a week, varying the foursomes each day to avoid getting on each other's nerves. That number has been reduced by death and infirmities to three.

Father McKnight was a devout Catholic priest, but he was also a devoted and expert golfer and a delightful man, full of fun, friendliness, mischief and quick wit. He was everyone's favorite, and he was my dear friend. Once I was 5 up on Father McKnight in an important senior match only to lose in extra holes. I went home despondent and seeking sympathy from my wife Ruth. When I told her what had happened, she said, "Oh! I think it's nice that Father won!"

On another occasion we played a match against each other in the Senior Club Championship. We were allowed by the powers-that-be to play the match at a time other than Super Sunday because the priest had other duties to perform on Sunday mornings. When I arrived on the first tee, I found a banner streaming across it reading, "The whole world wants Father McKnight to win". But he didn't.

After a heart attack left Father McKnight with a failing heart and precarious health, his bishop considered transferring him to another parish where he would be expected to build a new church. Father McKnight was comfortable in his little parish in Custer and was apprehensive over his proposed transfer. So I wrote a letter to his bishop explaining that the move would be hazardous to his life. The bishop was sympathetic and cancelled the order. Meanwhile I wrote a second letter for Father McKnight alone to see. It read in part, "He claims to be ill, but he sure looked healthy when he whipped me in the last tournament. How soon can you get him out of here?"

Sid McKnight, an Epworth member from Kansas City and no relation to the priest, was the president of Montgomery Ward and Co. and a director of Wal-Mart. He was a fine man, quiet and unassuming and good company on the golf course. When I played against him in a match one day, he holed a six-foot putt on the first green. I commented, "Sid, that's the finest putting stroke in the club!" As we walked off the green, Herman Yoder said to me out of the side of his mouth, "Isn't it a little early for that shit?" Sid never made a putt the rest of the day. He developed a terminal case of the yips that was painful to watch. Every two-footer was an adventure and an ordeal. But he was too proud to switch to the long putter.

Sid and the priest met for the first time on the sixteenth tee of the course one evening as they joined each other to play the last few holes. One of them put out his hand and said, "My name's McKnight." The other one replied, "So's mine!"

The most disastrous hole I ever played occurred when I was playing with my brother Bob, who was visiting from Iowa, and with Kim Berger. I got into the woods to the left on what is now the sixteenth and began rattling shots off the trees. One unfortunate ricochet hit Kim in the head, making a peculiar hollow sound. When I finally escaped the trees, my opponents were doubled over with laughter and they asked how many strokes I had taken. I said, "Fifteen!" They said, "We counted sixteen!"

This is reminiscent of the Scottish player who got involved with one of the pot bunkers at St. Andrews. When he was asked how many strokes he had taken, he replied, "I can only tell you that I went in at five minutes past twelve and got out at a quarter to one!"

In the old days, Kim Berger was the best putter I ever encountered. He had a hickory-shafted blade putter, and he could work magic with it, bringing the ball almost to a stop on the lip of the cup before it dropped in. One day he showed up with a metal-shafted putter. I said to him, "Kim, why are you doing this? You're already the best putter in the club!" He replied, "It might get better!" But it didn't. When he went back to the old putter, the magic was gone. Eventually the putter was broken by a caddy. Reshafting it was not successful, and Kim became as twitchy on the green as the worst of us, especially on two-footers. Members who played with him in later years would not believe that he had ever been a wizard on the greens.

There is one benefit of growing old in golf that I never counted on. The people with whom I play have been exceedingly helpful to me on the course. Dick Rathsack has been outstanding, but other companions have done much the same, replacing my divots, raking the sand, helping me in and out of bunkers, lifting my bag of clubs for me, and driving me as close as possible to my destination. It not only makes it possible for me to keep on playing, but it's heart-warming that people are so kind.

Once, when I was not so old and was still walking and carrying my own golf bag, I played golf with a man in New Zealand who was only two years younger than I was. I found the New Zealanders in general to be remarkably friendly, but this man was something special. He continually lifted my bag for me and helped me in other ways. When I asked him why he was doing these things, he replied that it was because he hoped that others would help him when he got old! I told him to forget it. The chances were that nobody would do anything for him at all.

CHAPTER XIX
IN SUMMARY

Familiarity breeds, if not contempt, at least a failure to fully appreciate what we have. In 1987 Hal Madden and I played golf with two Irish gentlemen at Ballybunion, an Irish golf course which was rated as the fifth best course in the world. After the round and over drinks I commented to these men that they were so lucky to be able to play this spectacular golf course every day. One of them replied, "We don't know that. This is the only course we've ever played!"

In the same way I think most of us do not fully appreciate what we have here. Last summer I played golf at Lincoln Hills with two friends from downstate. Both of these gentlemen, who play exceptional golf courses at home, lavishly praised both the layout and the conditioning of the Lincoln Hills golf course. The player from the Detroit area, who had also played the course many years before, said, "John, if this golf course were located near Detroit, neither of us could afford to belong to it!"

Three conditions would have to be met before Lincoln Hills would be considered to be among the great golf courses. First, it would have to be longer, especially in these modern times of high tech equipment. The course has been stretched as far as it can be, given the land and the original layout. But it plays longer than its yardage. We are used to seeing drives on television which roll 50 yards and even 100 yards after landing. We never see that at Lincoln Hills. In fact a few years ago, when the course was overwatered, it was not unusual for a good drive to hop backwards after landing.

The second condition would be to have more hazards. We have no water hole, although one was planned by the Matthews Company in their proposal of 1984. We have only 34 bunkers, and two holes have no bunkers at all. Having said this, the bunkers which we have are strategically located. Other more subtle problems lurk for the golfers in the form of uneven fairway lies, strategically placed trees, lush rough at the edges of the fairways, and long grass and tussocks in the second cut of rough.

The condition of this deeper rough is so extreme that it seems to have brought forth a new local descriptive word. We call it the "mahafka". I have never heard this word used at other clubs, so I suspect that it was invented here. It is generally used in a jocular or mocking way such as after your buddy has hit a duck hook, you tell him, "You are in the mahafka!", or to be redundant, "in the deep mahafka". I wondered if this word might have a Polish derivation meaning a field with long grass, but I questioned a Polish medical school classmate whose wife is also an expert in Balkan languages and they assured me that they have no such word.

The last condition which would have to be met for Lincoln Hills to be considered a great course is to have a famous sponsor. Ballybunion had only local prestige until Tom Watson played it and waxed lyrical over it. Crystal Downs had no national recognition until Ben Crenshaw "discovered" it as an old-style treasure.

Hundreds of people have been a part of the Lincoln Hills success story: the founders; the original architect; past presidents; greens chairmen; committee members; greens-keepers; and consultants. Names come into my mind like Fred Church, W. T. Culver, Pete Hardy, Henry Haskell, Bub Starke, Turk Matthews, and Tom Gatke. But if I had to pick one individual who accomplished the most and devoted himself to the club's benefit completely and for the longest time, I would have to pick Herman Yoder. The club was his chief hobby for at least forty years.

Lincoln Hills Golf Club has come a long way since its inception in 1920. There have been many changes, most of them for the better. We have spent many happy hours at Lincoln Hills, as well as some not so happy ones when the putter was balky or the drives were errant. It is our hope that the future directors of Lincoln Hills will maintain a sound financial policy that will enable the club to remain viable long after we are gone, so that new generations of golfers will be able to enjoy the same pleasures, thrills, and companionship that we have experienced over the last sixty years.

APPENDICES
A. TIMELINE OF EVENTS

1787	Northwest Ordinance establishes Michigan Territory and its boundaries.
1835	Stevens T. Mason is appointed Governor of the Michigan Territory. Ohio tries to steal Toledo and the port of the Maumee River.
1837	Michigan achieves statehood. Ohio gets Toledo.
1840	State of Michigan is apportioned into counties. Burr Caswell is first permanent settler in Mason County area.
1841-5	Charles Mears acquires tracts of land in the area. Lumbering begins.
1859	Hamlin Dam washes out.
1860	Mears changes the exit channel of Pere Marquette Lake.
1861	Name of city of Pere Marquette is changed to Ludington. County seat is moved from Buttersville to Lincoln.
1867	County seat is moved to Ludington.
1873	Flint and Northern Railroad comes to Mason County.
1887	St. Andrews Golf Club is established as the first golf club in the United States.
1888	Hamlin Dam is washed out devastating the town of Hamlin.
1892	Chicago Golf Club is established as the first midwestern golf club.
1894	Epworth Heights agrees to move its assembly to Ludington.
1895	Epworth League Railway is established.
1900	Epworth Golf Course is established. Railroad is renamed as the L&N Railroad.

1904-12 Michigan National Guard has summer training sessions at the Lincoln Fields.
1907 Troop train runs into Dummy Line. Paulina Stearns Hospital is established.
1909 Bridge is completed across Lincoln Lake. Epworth comes into possession of its grounds.
1910 Cartier Park is established.
1913 Ludington-Epworth Country Club clubhouse is built. Hamlin dam collapses again.
1912-14 Probable first nine hole golf course at the Lincoln Fields.
1915-18 U.S. Army begins Officers' training at Lincoln Fields.
1916 L&N Railroad acquires property through Epworth and Lincoln Hills.
1918 Army abandons Lincoln Fields. Leaves officers' quarters behind.
1919 Beautiful Ludington-Epworth Country Club clubhouse burns.
1921 Lincoln Hills Golf Club is established and opened.
1922 Epworth sues J.S. Stearns and the L&N Railroad to remove tracks.
1925 Lincoln Hills owns its own land.
1931 Lincoln Hills builds new clubhouse. Ludington Country Club is abandoned.
1932 M-116 is built.
1934 Ludington State park is opened.
1936 Epworth files unsuccessful application to ISCC to remove railroad tracks. Railroad is sold to Sargent Sand Co.
1937 Sargent Sand Co. begins operations.
1955 Lincoln Hills settles with bondholders, sells land, and builds first watering system.
1956 Lincoln Hills clubhouse is remodeled.
1959 Lincoln Hills Country Club Annex is installed
1984 Bruce & Jerry Matthews draw up long-range plan for Lincoln Hills.
1985 Old eighth green is redone.
1989 Lincoln Hills clubhouse is again remodeled.

1992 Railroad wins suit against Epworth over L&N property.
1997 Epworth purchases L&N right-of-way from railroad.
1998 Major remodeling of Lincoln Hills Golf course is undertaken.
2004 Lincoln Hills sues Epworth over right-of-way.
2006 Lincoln Hills and Epworth come to agreement over property between them.

Club members, L to R, Hal Madden, Dick Rathsack, John Carney, Bob Coury, and Chris Bentz welcome the opening of the course in 2003.

B. THE FOUNDING FATHERS OF LINCOLN HILLS

Abrahmson, Martin	President Abrahamson Nerheim Coal Co.
Alexander, C. N.	Epworth
Anderson, Arthur	President of Arthur Anderson Accounting, Epworth
Aschbacker, Karl L.	President Western Oil Co., Owner Toggery Clothing Founder WKLA Radio Station
Askew, F. J.	Epworth
Baltzer, George R.	Secretary/Treasurer Hammond Rohn Insurance Agency
Barber, W. C.	Epworth
Barthell, Ed E.	Attorney, Epworth
Buckley, F. C.	Epworth
Butler, L. E.	Epworth
Cantrell, D. H.	Epworth
Carroll, C. A.	Attorney/Appellate Judge, Epworth
Cornish, Ed	Epworth
Crawford, P. W.	Epworth
Culver, Wilmer T.	Vice-President, Carrom Co., L&N Railroad, & Haskell Boat Co.
Danaher, Michael B.	Vice-President, State Bank
Dillman, A. C.	Epworth
Drach, George O.	Owner of Dry Goods Store
Elliott, J. H.	
Estes, W. L.	Epworth
Gatke, Thomas L.	Gatke Brake Lining Co., Epworth
Garrard, Charles A.	Epworth
Gillett, W. N.	Epworth
Gnam, Charles	Epworth
Grundeman, Leo	Owner, City Bakery
Hamel, Alexander W.	President, Ludington Auto Sales, Lakeside Printing Co.
Hammond, W. L.	President, Hammond-Rohn Insurance Agency, Trustee, Stearns Estate

Hansen, H. C.	
Hardy, Elbert C.	Manager, Morton Salt Co.
Haskell, Henry L.	Founder, Haskell Boat Co. & the Carrom Co.
Heysett, F. William	Surgeon
Hesterman, Hugo F.	Epworth
Holocroft, Charles T.	Epworth
Hollenberg, F. B. T.	Epworth
Hussey, J. B.	
Huston, Harry V.	
Jagger, C. B.	Probate Judge
Keiser, Addison A.	Attorney
Knight, Ambrose	
Magmer, J. M.	
Mathias, D. R.	Epworth
Monroe, R. F.	
Monroe, R. O.	
Nerheim, Steffen	Vice-President, Abrahamson Nerheim Coal Co.
O'Leary, J. B.	Epworth
Pratt, Albert L.	Probation Officer
Punton, John	Epworth
Punton, John Jr.	Epworth
Quail, R.	
Reid, C. P.	Epworth
Rohn, Eugene C.	President, Hammond Rohn Insurance Agency
Scott, Conoway	Epworth
Sheldon, F. C.	Epworth
Sheldon, C. W.	Epworth
Small, Authur	
Smith, J. J.	Banker, Detroit
Snyder, John C.	Epworth
Stearns, Justus. S.	President, Stearns Motor co., Haskell Boat Co. & L&N RR
Stearns, R. L.	
Stillman, H. A.	Epworth
Stogsdell, R. R.	Epworth

Strawn, Theodore   Epworth
Thompson, Theo. A.   President, Thompson Cabinet Co.
Vorce, L. E.   Manager, National Grocer Co. & Owner
                        Coal & Coke Co.

Waltz, B. E.
Widmark, F. Oscar   Owner, Widmark Lumber Co.
Wilson, Fred G.
Wing, C. G.
Wollensack, H. P.

C. PAST PRESIDENTS OF LINCOLN HILLS GOLF CLUB

1921-23	Wilmer T. Culver
1923-34	Alfred W. Church
1935	Alexander W. Hamel
1936-37	Karl B. Matthews
1938-39	Otto A. Starke Jr.
1948-50	Truman L. Atkinson
1951-52	Dr. Charles Paukstis
1953-54	Edward O. Hansen
1955-56	Len Edmondson
1957-58	Herman Yoder
1959-60	Jack Rasmussen
1961-62	Roland E. Palmquist
1963-64	L. Kimball Berger
1965-66	William Garlock
1967-68	Fred Harrington
1969	Leonard Gavigan
1970	Robert Erickson
1971	Wesley E. Stevenson
1972	Richard Parliament
1973	Dr. Joseph Morris
1974	Richard Genter
1975	Elwyn Olmstead
1976	Harold Madden
1977	Al Bloomer
1978	Ralph Johnson
1979-80	Lee Schoenherr
1981	Howard Hawley
1982	Joseph Feutz
1983	Ralph Cerny
1984	John Carney, Jr.
1985	Jack Maskal
1986-87	Gerald R. Ponko, Jr.
1988-89	Clarence Hartman
1990	Mark Pehrson

THE HISTORY OF LINCOLN HILLS GOLF CLUB: One Man's Perspective

1991	Milan S. Reed II
1992	Richard Scott
1993	Greg Magee
1994	Donald Schierholt
1995	Paul J. Danielson
1996	David Tolley
1997-98	Helen DeBeck
1999	Michael Klemm
2000	Donald Janish
2001	Kenneth Rocco
2002	Marc Lenz
2006-08	Alex Zaydel
2004-05	Erik Vettergren
2003	William Mitchell

D. CLUB CHAMPIONS

	Men's	Women's
1922	J. Bussey	
1923	Edward Cornish, Jr.	
1924	Louis Montedonico	
1925	O. A. Starke, Jr.	
1926	Edward Cornish, Jr.	
1927	O. A. Starke, Jr.	
1928	O. A. Starke, Jr.	
1929	No Championship	
1930	K. B. Matthews	
1931	O. A. Starke, Jr.	
1932	O. A. Starke, Jr.	
1933-42	No Championships	
1943	Gordon Galloway	Mildred Langell
1944	O. A. Starke, Jr.	Mildred Langell
1945	O. A. Starke, Jr.	Edith Sterns
1946	O. A. Starke, Jr.	Viola Fuller
1947	O. A. Starke, Jr.	
1948	O. A. Starke, Jr.	Viola Fuller
1949	Russell Wilson	Faye Dorrell
1950	O. A. Starke, Jr.	Faye Dorrell
1951	Russell Wilson	Faye Dorrell
1952	O. A. Starke, Jr.	Helene Peterson
1953	O. A. Starke, Jr.	Barbara Rohn
1954	Russell Wilson	Faye Dorrell
1955	Louis Anderson	Helene Peterson
1956	Len Edmondson	Faye Dorrell
1957	Len Edmondson	Barbara Rohn
1958	O. A. Starke, Jr.	Barbara Rohn
1959	Len Edmondson	Barbara Rohn
1960	Walt Zbjoniewicz	Barbara Rohn
1961	Len Edmondson	Barbara Rohn
1962	John Goulet	Barbara Rohn
1963	James Tallefson	Barbara Rohn
1964	Len Edmondson	Helene Peterson

1965	O. A. Starke, Jr.	Barbara Rohn
1966	Lee Edmondson	Helene Peterson
1967	Lee Edmondson	Barbara Rohn
1968	Lee Edmondson	Barbara Rohn
1969	Lee Edmondson	Barbara Rohn
1970	Lee Edmondson	Barbara Rohn Harrington
1971	Charles Jury	Barbara Rohn Harrington
1972	Paul Kolinski	Barbara Rohn Harrington
1973	Paul Kolinski	Barbara Rohn Harrington
1974	Nate Graham	Barbara Rohn Harrington
1975	Dan Motyka	Barbara Rohn Harrington
1976	Paul Kolinski	Joanne May Shepard
1977	Paul Kolinski	Joanne May Shepard
1978	Charles Peterson	Barbara Rohn Harrington
1979	Dan Motyka	Barbara Rohn Harrington
1980	Charles Peterson	Barbara Rohn Harrington
1981	Charles Peterson	Barbara Rohn Harrington
1982	Dan Motyka	Carole Schierholt
1983	Dan Motyka	Carole Schierholt
1984	Paul Kolinski	Barbara Rohn Harrington
1985	Dan Motyka	Carole Schierholt
1986	Gerald R. Ponko. Jr.	Barbara Rohn Harrington
1987	Dan Motyka	Barbara Rohn Harrington
1988	Clayton Schaner	Carole Schierholt
1989	Dick Gretzinger	Carole Schierholt
1990	Dan Motyka	Barbara Rohn Harrington
1991	Greg Magee	Carole Schierholt
1992	Greg Magee	Barbara Rohn Harrington
1993	Greg Magee	Carole Schierholt
1994	Greg Magee	Carole Schierholt
1995	Dan Motyka	Dina Hackert
1996	Dick Gretzinger	Carole Schierholt
1997	Brian Boals	Carole Schierholt
1998	Brian Boals	Dina Hackert
1999	Gerald R. Ponko, Jr.	Dina Hackert
2000	Gerald R. Ponko, Jr.	Carole Schierholt
2001	Bill McPike	Dina Hackert
2002	Dick Gretzinger	Carole Schierholt

2003	Dan Motyka	Carole Schierholt
2004	Brian Boals	Carole Schierholt
2005	Dan Motyka	Carole Schierholt
2006	Dick Gretzinger	Carole Schierholt
2007	Dennis Tabor	Kim Dekker

THE TEN COMMANDMENTS OF GOLF
[for non-tournament play]

1] Play the ball as it lieth, except only if a] the fairway be uneven, b] the rough stony or with exposed roots, c] thou hast suffered a stroke, or d] thy handicap be more than 18.

2] Count all thy strokes unless a] they reacheth double figures and thy opponents do not, or b] thou art hopelessly out of the hole. In that case thou mayest take one more than thy worst opponent unless thou wishest to build up thy handicap.

3] If thy ball shouldst become lost, drop one in a nice playable spot reasonably near to where thou thinkest thy ball may have finished. Be gentle with thyself. Do not even thinkest of returning to the spot from which thou struckest thy last shot. Art thou mad, and doth thou wishest to hold up the entire course and incur the wrath of all other players?

4] If thy ball liest clearly outside the boundary lines of the course, thou shouldst drop a ball somewhere near where thy ball exited the course, adding a stroke, and making sure that thou hast a decent lie and a line to the green. Seest thou commandment 4 about going back to hit another.

5] Try to tee thy ball behind the markers, but if thou makest a small error, play on and ignorest thou the rude remarks which follow, and the reverse be true.

6] Shouldst thou mistakenly play a ball other than thine own, apologize and play thine own as if nothing hath happened, save that if thou hast struck thy opponent's ball into a hazard, it is proper to replace it with one of thine own, not too much less valuable than the lostie.

7] If thy opponent cheateth in thine eyes. Cast thine eyes elsewhere. Remember that that is how he gotteth his handicap.

8] Ignoreth thou the myriad of picky-picky and ticky-tacky rules of golf. If thou hadst wanted to work with these, thou wouldst have entered the Internal Revenue Service. God hateth a clubhouse lawyer.

9] Keepeth thou all wagers below the level where thou mayest become aggravated if thy opponent deviateth from what thou conceiveth as thy version of the Rules of Golf. Never under any circumstances call a penalty on thy opponent. Thou mayest help him to count his score, and thou mayest point out to him rules infractions, so that he may be better informed in the future. Remember that we are here to enjoy ourselves, not to suffer.

10] Play ready golf. Be ready when it is thy turn and if thy fellow be not ready, taketh his place. Rid thyself of all tics, twitches and rituals reminiscent of the mating dances of exotic birds. In short, hit the ball promptly and thy cup will runneth over with the gratitude of thy fellow players.

Made in the USA